THE ISLAMIC STATE DELUSION

GLEN SEGELL

Copyright © 2016 Glen Segell
The Islamic State Delusion
Glen Segell
All rights reserved.

Without limiting the rights under copyright reserved above, no part of this publication may be reproduced, stored in or introduced into a retrieval system, or transmitted, in any form or by any means (electronic, mechanical, photocopying, recording or otherwise), without the prior written permission of both the copyright owner and the publisher of the book.

Published in the United Kingdom by
The London Institute of Security Policy for Glen Segell

BM Letaba View
London, WC1N 3XX
United Kingdom

BISAC: Political Science, World, Middle Eastern

British Library Cataloguing in Publication Data
A catalogue record for this book is available from the British Library
All rights reserved.

ISBN: 1-901414-41-8
ISBN-13: 978-1-901414-41-7

DEDICATION

I wrote this book for Maya Glassman; because you are Maya, and are unique.
The Islamic State is a Delusion but you and your peace efforts are not Illusions.
Thank YOU.

CONTENTS

1	The Rise of the Islamic State	1
2	Accounting for Islamic State's Appeal and Resilience	10
3	Responding to Islamic State and Getting it Wrong	27
4	Fighting Islamic State: A Call to Action	49
5	Gazing into the Crystal Ball	61
	References	79

The Islamic State is a delusion, for had it been an illusion
I could and would have written:
Don't be dismayed at good-byes, a farewell is necessary before we meet again.
And meeting again, after moments or lifetimes, is certain for those who are friends.

1 THE RISE OF THE ISLAMIC STATE

Abstract

This chapter traces the origins of Islamic State to 1999 when Jordanian militant Abu Musab al-Zaraqawi established Al Qaeda in the Land of the Two Rivers. The renaming of the organization as the Islamic State of Iraq (ISI) was a turning point in that the organization saw itself not merely as a terrorist group wreaking revenge on American 'occupiers' but also as a governing entity. This chapter explores the structures of Islamic State and its strategic significance. The role of the Islamic State leader Caliph Al-Baghdadi is also examined. In conclusion we examine how Islamic State has managed to spread its influence into Africa, the Caucasus and the Far East.

Keywords: Abu Musab al-Zaraqawi, Caliph Al-Baghdadi, Al Qaeda, Islamic State of Iraq

Introduction

More than 20,000 people from 90 countries[1] have already flocked to Iraq and Syria to fight under the banner of the Islamic State (IS) and their self-styled "Caliph" Abu Bakr Al-Baghdadi[2] (whose real name is Ibrahim Badri al-Qurashi al-Sammarai). To put this into perspective – the pace at which this recruitment is occurring according to the US State Department is, *"greater than that at which foreign militants have gone to Afghanistan, Iraq, Yemen or Somalia at any point in the last 20 years"*[3]. The dangers that these pose are clearly evident in the recent terrorist atrocities in Australia, Canada, France and Libya. Indeed, the threat sleeper cells holds for national and global security cannot be under-estimated.

Despite an impressive international coalition aligned against IS, the jihadis have been getting stronger, spreading their tentacles across the Middle East west into Africa, and east into Asia. Away from the Islamic heartland, Islamic State is even acquiring recruits from the United States and across Europe. The tragic consequence of this recruitment is seen in the January 2015 attack on the offices of *Charlie Hebdo* in Paris. Clearly then, the current counter-terrorism strategies are failing. In order to understand the reasons for the failure of current strategies, we need to understand the nature of the threat posed by IS, as well as explore its organizational structure, its goals, strategies and tactics. It will be argued that current counter-terrorism constructs – based as it is on the nation-state and national security, are woefully inadequate to effectively respond to a global threat constituted by IS.

Origins of Islamic State: What's in a Name?

The origins of what developed into IS can be traced to 1999 when a Jordanian militant Abu Musab al-Zaraqawi established Al Qaeda in the Land of the Two Rivers (Euphrates and Tigris) which proved too cumbersome. The name was then shortened to Al Qaeda in Iraq (AQI) (*TanzimQa'idat al-Jihad fi Bilad al Rafidayn*) and in 2004, this group formally pledged allegiance to Al Qaeda[4]. By 2006 the group renamed itself as the *MajlisShura al-Mujahideen*. Later that year, and following the death of Al-Zarqawi it renamed itself as the Islamic State of Iraq or ISI (*Dawlat al-Iraq al-Islamiya*) under the leadership of Abu Omar al-Baghdadi[5]. The constant renaming of the organization suggests a movement in search of their own unique identity and something to distinguish themselves from other militant jihadi organizations in Iraq and further afield.

The naming of the organization as an "Islamic State" was the first indication that the objectives of the militant group had become more grandiose – that it saw itself as a governing entity. This notion of being a governing authority witnessed a "cabinet" announcement by the ISI in April 2007. Accordingly various "ministries" were created including a Ministry for Media Affairs, a Ministry for War, an Oil Ministry, a Ministry for Agriculture and Fisheries and a Ministry for Health. In addition to these "ministries" and given the religious zealotry guiding the actions of ISI, various Shar'ia Committees[6] were also created to apply and enforce Islamic law. It is important, too, to understand how sophisticated the nascent Islamic State had become in their strategic thinking. These "ministries" with staffed with technocrats such as a medical doctor, Dr. Abu Abdullah al-Zaidi, heading the Health Ministry and an engineer Abu Ahmad al-Janabi leading the Oil Ministry. Many Middle Eastern societies are tribal in nature.

Recognizing this, IS ensured that the cabinet were as inclusive as possible – reflecting the tribal mix of Iraqi society. The "Minister" of Media Affairs, for instance hailed from a Sunni area just north of Baghdad and was a Mashhadani, whilst his counterpart heading the Ministry of Martyrs and Prisoners was an Issawi from Anbar Province[7]. Governing in an inclusive manner (at least as far as Sunni Muslims were concerned) stood in sharp contrast to the lack of inclusive governance demonstrated on the part of the regime in Baghdad – or Damascus - for that matter.

Another very important ISI-created structure is a da'wah office. This office is often regarded as the bedrock of the organization given the multiplicity of roles it plays. First, it has a social outreach function specifically preaching their version of "pure Islam" to Muslims. As such it directly liaises with local mosques. The da'wah office's social outreach function also takes the form of erecting billboards calling on women to dress modestly and the like. This office also serves to recruit members as well as to collect intelligence on rival groups in the areas they occupy. It is also the da'wah office who liaises with community members if they have problems regarding the conduct of individual IS members[8]. Education, too, in a particular area falls under the purview of the da'wah office. Under the circumstances, it is not an exaggeration to state that the da'wah office is the building block of local administration and IS power in a given area.

Given the ongoing civil war in Syria which began in 2011 and the resultant political vacuum created, the organization soon established itself there prompting a name change once again in 2013 – the Islamic State in Iraq and Greater Syria (*Al Dawla al-Islamiya fil Iraq wa al-Sham* or ISIS). With increasing confidence of its global reach, ISIS saw itself as a global caliphate and renamed itself in 2014 simply as the Islamic State (IS)[9]. The new name suggests two things. First, that there are no geographic boundaries. Second, "the" implies that it is singular, the only Islamic State – one to which all 1.5 billion Muslims owes loyalty to. This was made empathically clear when Al-Baghdadi announced, "*Rush O Muslims to your State. Yes, it is your state. Rush, because Syria is not for the Syrians, and Iraq is not for the Iraqis*"[10]. Here then was a state which knew no territorial boundaries and encompassed 1.5 billion Muslims wherever they were. With the Declaration of a caliphate in June 2014[11], IS restructured itself to reflect itself as a state with various government departments operating at "national", "provincial" and "local" levels. As of August 2015, the IS "cabinet" is as follows:

Government Department	Function
Diwan al-Ta'lim	Education
Diwan al-Khidamat	Public Services (e.g. electricity,

	water, street cleaning). Management of public facilities (e.g. parks)
Diwan al-Rikaz	Precious resources (two known divisions: fossil fuels and antiquities)
Diwan al-Da'wahwa al-Masajid (wa al-Awqaf)	Da'wah activity and control of the mosques
Diwa al-Sihha	Health
Diwan al-Asha'ir	Tribal outreach
Diwan al-Amn (al-Aam)	Public security
Diwan Bayt al-Mal	Finances and currency system
Diwan al-Hisbah	Enforcement of public morality: Islamic police
Diwan al-Qadawa al-Mazalim	Islamic court, judicial matters, marriages
Diwan al-Alaqat al-Amma	Public relations
Diwan al-Zira'a	Agriculture, environment
Diwan al-Ifta' wa al-Buhuth	Fatwas, textbooks for training camp recruits, etc
Diwan al-Jund	Military and defence

Table 1: Diwans and their Functions[12]

Militarily, IS has its origins in post-Saddam Hussein Iraq with AQI battling the American presence as well as Iraqi Shi'a and Iranian domination[13]. The relationship between AQI and Al Qaeda central however soured quite quickly given major tensions over doctrine and tactics. On doctrine, Al Qaeda was concerned about AQI's understanding of the Islamic doctrine of *takfir* which is when a Muslim is declared to be an apostate[14]. AQI's rather broad interpretation of what constituted such heresy resulted in them killing other Muslims in the region they controlled. Al Qaeda central was concerned that this wouldserve to alienate Iraqi public opinion. It should be borne in mind that the Baathist part in Iraq (and Syria) was secular in nature. Consequently the phenomenon of non-practicing Muslims was common in Saddam Hussein's Iraq. The doctrine of *takfir*, then, Al Qaeda central feared, would render large numbers of Iraqis hostile towards AQI.

Tactically, too, there were differences specifically as it related to the ambitions between AQI and its parent body. Vengeance largely is what drove Al Qaeda, to give the Americans and other "occupiers" a bloody nose in Iraq, AQI's agenda was far more ambitious seeking not mere revenge but to govern the areas they controlled under Islamic shar'ia law like a state[15]. The tensions between these two organizations grew to such an extent that Al Qaeda cut off all ties with the group in February 2014[16].

Caliph Al-Baghdadi

Al-Baghdadi's growing Islamism and Sunni-biased sectarianism began during his academic days as a student at the University for Islamic Sciences where he eventually earned his doctorate. As a student he was active in Iraq's Muslim Brotherhood. By 2000 his Islamist ideological convictions led him to join a Sunni militant group – the Jaysh al-Mujahideen (or Army of the Mujahideen). With the US occupation of Iraq in 2003, he formed his own Islamist grouping - the JayshAhl al-Sunnah wa al-Jammah (the Army of the People of the Sunni Community)[17]. His militant armed group was active in eastern Iraq fighting the US-led "invasion".

He was eventually captured by US forces in 2005 and was sent to a prison camp in southern Iraq – Bucca. Here he made contact with other AQI fighters also imprisoned at Bucca[18]. Reflecting on his time at Bucca, Michael Weiss and Hassan Hassan[19] notes,

"His PhD in Islamic Studies conferred a jusrisprudential wisdom on him to which squabbling jihadist inmates seemed to defer. As such, the Americans let him travel among the different camp blocs at Bucca, ostensibly to resolve conflicts; instead, al-Baghdadi used the indulgence to recruit more foot soldiers".

He consolidated his power base in prison and many of his fellow inmates here were later to become his lieutenants in IS. Following his release from prison, he remained active within AQI. Following the deaths of al-Zaraqawi and his successors – Abu Omar al- Baghdadi and Abu Hamza al-Muhajir; in May 2010, the Shura Council of AQI appointed Abu Bakr al-Baghdadi to the leadership position[20]. His ascent to leadership of AQI was at a time when AQI was rudderless and were suffering one military setback after another[21].

However, Al-Baghdadi was astute enough to recognize an opportunity when he witnessed the civil war raging in neighbouring Syria – it opened the door for AQI into Syria[22]. As a result, in 2011 Al-Baghdadi dispatched one of his key lieutenants, Abu Muhammed al-Jowlani who was a Syrian national together with a number of ISI operatives into Syria to expand the organization there. From this Syrian operation emerged Jabhat al-Nusra[23]. With the movement into Syria, al-Baghdadi increasingly saw ISI as a nascent global Islamic state or caliphate. Needless to say tensions escalated between Al Qaeda and al-Baghdadi. By June 2013, al-Baghdadi was confident enough to reject both Al Qaeda and the leadership of Ayman al-Zawahiri[24]. Later that same month, on the 29th June 2014, IS proclaimed itself a worldwide caliphate with al-Baghdadi as its leader[25]. It is also clear that Abu Bakr al-Baghdadi's claim that he is a member of the Quraysh tribal confederation[26] from which the prophet of Islam stems as well that he is a direct descendant of the prophet Muhammad[27] was also to give his ascent to the caliphate greater legitimacy. These claims also sought to portray al-Baghdadi higher in rank than Al Qaeda's al-Zawahiri. To put it differently, then the severing off ties by al-Zawahiri in February 2014, was then a mere formality since the actual decision was taken by al-Baghdadi eight months previously. Following the schism between Al Qaeda and IS, Jabhat al-Nusra remained loyal to Al Qaeda and would become a thorn in the side of IS when it moved into Syria.

Islamic State spreads its Tentacles

IS currently controls territory in Iraq and Syria the size of Britain with a population of 10 million. Within their territory they have an army, police force and a judicial system and an annual budget of approximately US $2 billion[28]. To all intents and purposes, IS has *de facto* control over a 'state' within the borders of two *de jure* states – Iraq and Syria. It is important to understand that in creating this state, Al Baghdadi has directly challenged the colonial arrangements which most Arabs view as humiliating. The colonial borders as per the 1916 Sykes-Picot Agreement resulted in minorities regimes governing Iraq and Syria. Minority Sunnis were in control over Shia-majority Iraq whilst minority Alawites, a branch of Shi'ism, dominated the Sunni majority in Syria. Andrew Phillips[29] examined the significance of this Islamist proto-state spanning the borders of Iraq and Syria,

"In attempting to consolidate a jihadist statelet spanning parts of Syria and Iraq, IS challenges the territorial dispensation that has prevailed since the 1916 Sykes-Picot Agreement first split the region into British and French spheres of influence. Sykes-Picot stands as an enduring symbol of betrayal and humiliation for the Arab world. Its prominence in IS propaganda reflects Al Baghdadi's canny marshalling of pan-Arabist sentiment to legitimate his fledgling statelet".

It is also important to recognize that IS views itself as a global, not regional caliphate. This is the true significance of the change of its name from IS to the Islamic State – it recognizes no geographical boundary. One IS statement clearly articulated the primacy of the IS caliphate over all other Islamist groupings, the world over, *"The legality of all emirates, groups, states and organizations become null by the expansion of the khilafah's [caliphate's] authority and arrival of its troops to their areas"*[30].

IS has already made some way headway towards these global ambitions having established sleeper cells in over 60 countries[31]. Throughout 2015, the terrorist group has spread its tentacles into the Muslim-inhabited Caucuses region as well as Indonesia, which is the largest Muslim country in the world as well as the Philippines and Thailand[32]. The militant movement has been quite adept in inserting itself into the Buddhist-Muslim tensions inside Thailand and Christian-Muslim rift in the Philippines. As a result both Thailand and the Philippines have Muslim separatist agitating for independence. The strategy seems to be paying dividends. At least 200 Indonesians and 150 Malaysians have joined IS. Some analysts have argued that there is enough of a support base in Indonesia for IS to quickly set up a structure there to target Jakarta[33] itself. In the case of their Caucasus strategy, several thousand IS fighters emanate from the northern Caucasus. 400 Chechens alone, have been killed in Iraq and Syria whilst fighting for IS[34].

IS has also given birth to local franchises, especially within the African context. Across the Sahel, and North Africa, local IS franchises are emerging. Two groups have split from al Qaeda in the Islamic Maghreb (AQIM) pledging their allegiance to Al--Baghdadi. In Algeria, AQIM commander Grouri Abdelmalik aka Khaled Abu Suleimane announced that he and his troops were breaking away from AQIM which according to him had `deviated from the true path' and established themselves as the Jund al-Khilafah or Soldiers of the Caliphate. He made clear that this new grouping was now aligned to IS. Posting a communique on jihadi websites, Abdelmalik addresses the self-styled caliph of IS, Abu Bakr al-Baghdadi, *"You have in the Islamic Maghreb men if you order them they will obey you"*[35]. In Morocco an IS cell was discovered in the city of Meknes and in the Northern Rif mountains in the towns of El-Hajeb and El- Hoceima two more active IS cells was discovered. More ominously one Moroccan official noted that nearly 2000 Moroccans are currently fighting alongside IS in Iraq and Syria[36]. This, of course, raises the troubling question of what happens when these Moroccan fighters return home. Similar developments are also occurring in Tunisia where the Uqba Ibn Nafi Brigade also split from AQIM and pledged their allegiance to IS[37]. In strife-torn Libya, meanwhile, returning jihadis from Syria have established the al-Battar Brigade[38].

Meanwhile, in the Sinai, the Islamists of Ansar Beit al-Maqdis have also declared their allegiance to al-Baghdadi[39]. In July 2015, an affiliate of Ansar Bayt al-Maqdis – the Sinai Province Group carried out simultaneous assaults on numerous army checkpoints in the Sinai Peninsula[40] which resulted in several Egyptian soldiers killed and scores more wounded. Interestingly the group received support from Gaza's Hamas in the form of weapons and logistical support. Wael Faraj, a senior commander of Hamas' armed wing also smuggled wounded IS-affiliated fighters from the Sinai to Gaza ostensibly for medical treatment[41]. This demonstrates how IS can read a situation to draw maximum benefit for itself. Hamas, was closely associated with Egypt's Muslim Brotherhood but when it was deposed from power and President al-Sisi came to power in 2013 – relations between Cairo and Hamas soured[42]. Understanding these tensions, IS affiliates' used it to maximum effect thereby using Hamas to assist their offensive on the Sinai Peninsula.

Islamic State, is however, ultimately loyal to itself and if it believes that it can supplant its local partner, it would gladly do so. During October 2015, clashes erupted between Israeli security forces and Palestinians at Al Aqsa Mosque in Jerusalem – the third holiest site in Islam after Mecca and Medina. Following a spate of stabbings of Israeli Jews, Israeli security services adopted harsh security measures. At least 41 Palestinians and eight Israelis were killed and scores injured in the first three weeks of October 2015[43]. IS quickly put out videos aimed to incite more attacks congratulating Palestinians for the stabbings and urged them to turn Jews "...*into rotten corpses and scattered body parts*"[44]. IS various social media outlets also attacked the Palestinian leadership. Fatah, in control of the West Bank, and because of its moderation was declared the "...*agent of the infidel Jews and Christians*", whilst Islamic State's ally Hamas was not radical enough and was doing the "...*bidding of the Shi'ites [Iranians] and Alawites [the Syrian regime]*"[45]. Not satisfied with its small but significant present on the Gaza Strip, Islamic State, is clearly attempting to hijack the Palestinian cause for itself and create a rival to both Fatah and Hamas[46].

Beyond buying into the global caliphate ideology of IS, local groups such as Nigeria's Boko Haram which have pledged an oath of allegiance to Al-Baghdadi[47] also make a rational choice that their allegiance would translate into greater military assistance and greater funds. After all, many former Baathists of the Saddam Hussein regime, specifically their Republican Guards have gone on to bolster IS' ranks[48]. Two of Al-Baghdadi's senior deputies are Abu Ali al-Anbari, a former Major-General in Saddam Hussein's army who is in charge of all IS operations in Syria and Abu Muslim al-Turkmani, a former Colonel in Saddam Hussein's military intelligence. He continues to play this role for IS[49].It is these former Baathist officers which have come to play a significant role in Islamic State's military successes. It is they who train new IS recruits. It is they who direct IS' intelligence apparatus. It is they who plan its military strategy[50].

These skills, in turn, have been lent out to local IS franchises such as Boko Haram which, in turn, has seen an exponential rise in their military professionalism and the sophistication in which they have displayed when mounting attacks. Funds, which IS has access to, meanwhile can greatly finance Boko Haram's own regional ambitions. In the immediate short-term, Boko Haram's leader Abubaker Shekau has already benefited from his allegiance to the IS leader. Boko Haram, for instance, is already benefiting from shared intelligence and tactics as well as materiel support from IS[51]. The requisite military skills and funds from IS also came at a time when Boko Haram was coming under intense military pressure. In February 2015 a major military offensive again Boko Haram positions by Nigerian and West African forces resulted in Boko Haram losing 25 towns. The following month, in March 2015, Abubaker Shekau took an oath of allegiance to Abu Bakr al-Baghdadi[52]. A case, can therefore be made, that this was desperate opportunism on the part of Boko Haram – essentially turning to IS to save it from certain military defeat. Al Baghdadi, in turn, accepted this oath of allegiance and promptly renamed Boko Haram as the Islamic State's Wilayat West Africa[53]. In addition, the IS leadership immediately made contact with Ansaru – a faction of Boko Haram who took issue with Shekau's leadership style – urging them to reintegrate with the main body of Boko Haram. With the two factions of Boko Haram now united, expect there to be more vicious terrorist attacks in Nigeria and the West African region[54]. Moreover, with the expansion of the Islamic State Wilayat Libya, there may be a real possibility that IS' franchises in West and North Africa could link up with serious implications for regional security.

The success Islamic State has undoubtedly had necessitates a serious assessment of its resilience, its appeal, its strategy and tactics. Understanding this may be a key to design more effective counter-terrorism strategies.

2 ACCOUNTING FOR ISLAMIC STATE'S APPEAL AND RESILIENCE

Abstract

Despite having a vast number of forces arrayed against it – the US coalition, Putin's Moscow, Iran and its proxy Hezbollah, Kurdish Peshmerga and the regimes in Baghdad and Damascus, Islamic State is growing stronger. Reasons for the resilience displayed on the part of the jihadis include encouraging polarization between groups and then benefiting from this process, its diverse funding sources from oil sales to the trafficking of antiquities and narcotics has allowed it to build a war chest in excess of US$ 2billion. With these funds, Islamic State has deployed soft power – digging sewage systems, providing stipends to families, to earn the loyalty of its "citizens". Islamic State has also displayed superior military strategy combining conventional military doctrine with asymmetric warfare.

Keywords: Iraqi Special Forces, Kurdish Peshmerga, social media, funding, soft power

Introduction

One of the major reasons accounting for the failure of current counter-terrorism efforts against IS jihadis is that they are under-estimated. In fact, IS demonstrates sophisticated command of tactics and strategy – from military and psychological warfare to their exploits on social media. Moreover, IS has demonstrated an ability to adapt its tactics and in a fast-evolving environment, exploiting its enemies' weaknesses and ensuring that it does not play to its enemies strengths. In addition, accurately predicting its foes responses, IS ensures that these responses work towards their broader strategy. As was explained in Chapter 1, Islamic State is not merely a terrorist organization and insurgency. It is also a *de* facto state and has access to political and economic instruments to bolster its nascent state. To understand its appeal and resilience, then we need to explore its political instruments (increasing polarisation and sectarian strife, its deployment of soft power and its social media outreach), economic instruments especially as it pertains to funding and administering its state and its military strategy and tactics.

Political Instruments: Increasing polarization and sectarian strife

The overall politicalstrategy of IS seems to want to increase polarization and sectarian tensions as seen by the gruesome execution videos it routinely posts online of killings of Yazidis, Christians and the like whilst at the same time targeting those Muslims of a moderate disposition. Clearly, IS believes that it can only stand to benefit from the growing polarization in society as in the words of the Brazilian revolutionary Carlos Marighela, the "soft centre"[55] would be eliminated. Following the barbaric attack on the Charlie Hebdo offices in Paris in January 2015[56] a wave of Islamophobia has swept Europe which was intensified by another IS-inspired attack on Copenhagen in February 2015[57]. In Dresden, Germany, for instance a group calling itself the Patriotic Europeans against the Islamification of the West (PEGIDA) soon spread to other cities in Germany like Cologne, Hamburg, Munster and Stuttgart bringing tens of thousands of people on the streets in anti-Islam rallies. This has been replicated in other European capitals[58]. Following the multiple terror attacks in France in November 2015, Islamophobia again increased across Europe[59].This Islamophobia is bound to antagonize an already alienated European Muslim community[60] - hundreds of whom have already left to join IS. According to David von Drehle[61] the number of European Muslims who have fought in Syria and Iraq, include:

France – 1200
United Kingdom – 600
Germany – 500-600
Belgium – 440
Netherlands – 200-250
Sweden – 150-180
Denmark – 100-150
Austria – 100-150
Spain – 50-100
Italy – 80
Finland – 50-70

Norway – 60
Switzerland – 40
Ireland – 30

The return of these trained jihadis to their respective countries has also served to increase European citizens' security anxieties. Moreover, given the tens of thousands of migrants fleeing IS from Syria, Iraq and other countries into Europe, it has created the perfect opportunity for IS to infiltrate the masses of genuine refugees with their own trained operatives to wreak havoc in Europe. Given the waves of desperate humanity at their doors, many European countries did not have the opportunity to go through the necessary security checks of each and every migrant allowed into the European Union. In some instances even rudimentary checks like photographing and taking the fingerprints of these migrants were not done. Under the circumstances, Aaron Brown[62] estimates that IS has 4,000 covert gunmen already in Europe which they have smuggled amongst the refugees. The resultant fear amongst Europeans, in turn, has only served fan the flames of Islamophobia further.

A similar hardening of attitudes is taking place across the Atlantic, in the United States which has witnessed increased terrorist activity. On the 3rd May 2015, for instance, there was an IS – inspired assault on a Prophet Muhammed cartoon contest in Garland, Texas. The two individuals involved, Elton Simpson and Nadir Hamid Soofi, were in contact with IS. Simpson, it was subsequently discovered, was in Twitter contact with Muhammed Abdullahi Hassan aka MujahidMiski – an IS recruiter from Minneapolis[63]. By the end of 2014, 100 Americans had gone to Syria to join Islamic State[64]. Unsurprisingly, the US public is increasingly viewing Muslims as a threat. According to the Pew Research Centre 42 percent of Americans say Islam is more likely than other religions to incite violence amongst its followers[65]. From a strategic perspective, the attack on Garland gave fresh insights into IS' strategy and the challenge to policy makers. Whilst the militant group's Bayan Radio claimed responsibility for the attack and threatened Americans that *"what is coming will be worse and more bitter"*[66], it is also clear that neither of the two assailants – Simpson and Soofie – received financial or military assistance from IS nor discussed their plans or even sought permission from IS. Rather, Daniel Pipes[67] astutely observes that IS does not plan or direct its attacks on Western targets. Rather, it leverages its high profile to incite Muslims against their non-Muslim neighbours. In other words, its aims to inspire attacks not plan or organize them. This perspective was reinforced when 24 year-old Mohammod Youssuf Abdulazeez killed five servicemen in Chattanooga, Tennessee and injured two others when he opened fire on an armed services recruiting centre and a military training facility[68].

In 2014, IS also inspired such "lone-wolf" attacks in Ottawa, Canada and Sydney, Australia[69]. Whilst IS then runs a more centrally organized leadership in Iraq and Syria, its leadership is more decentralized outside of the territory it controls. What inspires such lone-wolf attacks is its political ideology – a narrative of alleged grievances[70] and a promise of a glorious future. This makes it extremely difficult for intelligence services to disrupt – the planning and organization is done at an individual level. This is highlighted in the case of Simpson.Despite the fact that he was under surveillance by authorities for over a year; the attack on Garland could not be thwarted before the event actually took place. This raises interesting questions as to what is actionable intelligence and legal questions as to when a suspect could be apprehended.

What takes primacy in such terrorist attacks is not the magnitude of the terrorist attack itself, but rather the ability to terrorize a population. As insecurity, fear and anxiety grows, so too does Islamophobia. This Islamophobia, in turn, Muslim disenchantment with Western societies and ultimately leads to more recruits into the Islamist cause.

Political Instruments: Islamic State's Deployment of `Soft Power'

IS also understands that capturing territory is only one aspect of a total strategy; that in order to hold that territory they also need to earn the trust of residents by providing basic services. IS jihadists have therefore fixed power lines, painted sidewalks, run regular bus services, removed expired food from markets, dug sewage systems, and re-opened luxury hotels and offered three free nights with all meals included for newlyweds. In addition, they have started manufacturing prosthetic limbs for the wounded and provided rudimentary, if brutal security, to inhabitants of the nascent state they control[71].

IS also established Islamic Services Committees to administer electricity supply, health spending, education, the cleaning of streets and the provision of food[72]. Following the capture of Palmyra in Syria, IS also embarked on winning the loyalties of citizens by freeing prisoners at the notorious Tadmur Prison. This had huge symbolic significance since it was here where political dissidents of the Assad regime were not only imprisoned but tortured. Since the start of the rebellion against Assad, the rebellion took on a distinct Sunni flavour. As a result, Tadmur Prison hosted many Sunni Islamists, including those of the Muslim Brotherhood. By freeing these prisoners, IS styled itself as the champion of Sunni interests against the ruling minority Alawite sect as represented by the Assad regime[73].

Islamic State is cognizant of the fact that both Iraq and Syria remain intensely tribal societies. Given the weakening of Baghdad and Damascus's control, tribal authorities have increasingly become more prominent in these conditions of state contraction. Recognizing this truism, IS has established an emir in charge of tribal affairs – Dhaigham Abu Abdullah – a Saudi national[74]. This was an inspired choice – utilizing a Saudi national to co-ordinate with and arbitrate between tribes as opposed to an Iraqi or Syrian national who would belong to one of the tribes and would therefore be open to accusations of bias. IS has co-opted tribal sheikhs through the use of various incentives. These include smuggling of contraband and dispensing gray-market rights[75]. In return, IS expected these sheikhs' unswerving loyalty.

In addition, recognizing that fratricidal conflict was not in the best interests of their nascent state, IS has acted as mediator between tribes. For instance, in the Syrian town of Albu Kamal, there have been tensions between the al-Hassoun and the al-Rehabiyeen tribes for thirty years. In November 2014 IS deftly mediated in the dispute – affecting reconciliation between the elders of the two tribes to the relief of all in the town[76]. There have been times; however, where Islamic State positions came under attack by tribal militias jealous of their autonomy being eroded by Islamic State. Recognizing that if they use their forces from pro-Islamic State tribes to take on the hostile tribe, it would merely lead to more tit-for-tat fighting which would undermine cohesion within the territory of IS, the jihadists pitted members of the same tribe against each other. In August 2014, for example, IS got members of the Shaitat tribe in Deir Ezzor to turn on other members of their own tribe which resulted in hundreds being killed. They accomplished this by means of supporting a younger generation of ambitious tribal leaders to turn against the older generation through the provision of funds and arms[77].

Islamic State also favours a fairly autonomous form of provincial governance. Under each province, local government are semi-autonomous as well. In practice, this means that "...*local populations can effectively control their own economies through Shura [consultative] councils and are therefore more likely to respond positively and remain loyal to their new rulers*"[78]. The ability to control your own affairs at the local level stands in sharp contrast to the over-centralizing, ineffective and draconian rule emanating from the Iraqi and Syrian governments. Moreover, in deeply sectarian societies such local governments can actually serve to minimise tensions between different groups. Even from a military standpoint, this provincial form of governance has advantages. It means that IS has active military units throughout the state it controls, that it has citizens willing to fight for it and/or support the military and that IS can now fight on multiple fronts simultaneously[79].

As a result, they have won over the much of the populace they control who compared them favourably with the neglect or oppression emanating from the Damascus and Baghdad governments. This would make the group harder to dislodge in future. IS also ensures the loyalty of their 31,000 fighters (as of January 2015)[80] by also involving the entire family unit. Whilst, fighters receive US $100 per month, another US $100 also goes towards the parents and each of the fighters' siblings receives US $40 per month. As Ben Hubbard[81] has noted it is a strategy designed to win over the entire family.

Political Instruments: Islamic State and Social Media

It is easy to understand the attraction to IS and the corresponding disenchantment of younger militants with Al Qaeda with its ageing leadership and its inability carry out a single major attack against the West. By contrast, IS through its slick recruitment videos displays that it has carved out a large swathe of territory in Iraq and Syria and its military successes in spite of Western airstrikes is appealing to a younger generation of would-be jihadis. Moreover social media also allows it to be in constant communication with its constituency and also allows IS to attract people outside of its cause as would be seen in a subsequent chapter by growing numbers of non-Muslims converting and joining the jihadis.

A key to the growth of IS, then, remains their ability to spread their ideology through the technologically savy approach to social media propaganda – Facebook, Twitter, You Tube and Instagram[82]. By March 2015, IS had 90,000 Twitter accounts to spread their propaganda and recruit new jihadis[83]. Just their English-language Twitter accounts have more than 21,000 followers – the majority of these concentrated in the West[84]. Islamic State also makes extensive use of Zello. This is an encrypted application for mobile devices which facilitates the sharing of audio messages. IS utilizes this platform to distribute its religious sermons to a younger generation tired of traditional sermons given by established and establishment clerics[85]. IS members extoll the virtue of such social media in shaping the narrative on IS and therefore influencing the public perception of the organization. *"Don't hear about us, hear from us,"* was the popular refrain amongst these IS members when discussing their social media outreach[86]. Nasser Balochi, a senior member of Islamic State's social media team, could not stressed the importance of social media enough when he declared, *"This is a war of ideologies as much as it is a physical war. And just as the physical war must be fought on the battlefield, so too must the ideological war be fought in the media"*[87].

The use of rap music in their recruitment videos is especially appealing to young alienated youth and is a far cry from the staid videos in which the older generation of Al Qaeda jihadis like Osama bin Laden and Ayman al Zawahiri appeared in. IS videos instead of focusing in on sermons from al-Baghdadi as was the case of Al Qaeda's leadership-centred videos rather focus on the "relatability" factor focusing on the IS rank-and-file. In addition, military successes with slick production techniques was the order of the day in these IS videos where a seductive narrative merged with powerful iconography[88].

Cori Dauber and Mark Robinson of the University of North Carolina noted in a recent paper the sophisticated visual techniques utilized by IS to enhance the quality of their propaganda videos. These range from *"…choosing starkly contrasting colours – think black uniforms and orange jumpsuits – to the use of multiple cameras, tight focus, "subjective" angles and intimate sounds to create an eyewitness effect"*[89]. The care with which the terrorist group has approached its social media outreach suggests that it understands social media's value in its communication and recruitment efforts. Beyond the quality of its postings, the sheer quantity is breath-taking. In a single week, IS produces 123 media releases in 6 languages, 24 of which were videos[90].

Not all these videos extol violence graphically depicting the decapitation of enemies of the "caliphate". Whilst a fair number do demonstrate this, many others articulate well-worn Muslim grievances against the West as well as eulogising the virtues of the Islamic State; them building schools and operating clinics in the areas they control. In the process, they articulate a concrete an alternative vision to the purported corrupt, secular, Western-oriented state. In other words, they put forth a vision of a caliphate where full shar'ia law is practiced as a concrete reality[91]. This has proved alluring. As Elizabeth Whitman[92] has observed recruits do not emanate only from those with militant backgrounds but is increasingly attractive to middle class Muslims who find the idea of a place where shar'ia law is applied in its purest form appealing. Of course, there is historical precedent to this. Consider an earlier generation of radicals who was seduced by Communism. Ernesto "Che" Guevara, medical doctor turned revolutionary, epitomises this trend. We will revisit this point later in this book.

In addition to more generic videos, Islamic State is quite adroit at creating videos for targeting specific constituencies and exploiting grievances of that community[93]. In addition to recruitment via social media[94], IS has also made use of targeted recruitment via family networks. This was certainly the case of the Portsmouth 5. Five British Muslims from the town of Portsmouth, was recruited by means of an IS recruiter, 25 year-old Ifthekar Jaman, who was a cousin of AsadUzzaman – one of the Portsmouth 5[95].

As was outlined earlier, the aim of such aggressive social media presence is not only for IS to put forward it message but also to inspire lone-wolf terrorism as we witnessed in Garland and Tennessee. US Federal Bureau of Investigation (FBI) Director James B. Comey refers to this as "crowdsource terrorism" where thousands of messages are generated each month encouraging Americans to launch attacks inside the US[96]. Worryingly, the FBI has acknowledged that there are hundreds of investigations open in all 50 US states into individuals who have been receiving messages from IS and who may decide to act on such instigation[97]. IS videos of extreme acts of violence, so graphically illustrated in its sadistic images of decapitations also serves the purpose to terrify its enemies whilst instilling into its followers a sense of omnipotence[98].

Thanks in part to persuasive social media, the penetration of IS ideology[99] even in far-away South Africa is seen in the writings of an 18-year-old South African from Johannesburg using the pseudonym of Abu Huraya al-Afriki who stated, *"I joined the Islamic State because their aim is to establish the world of Allah (There is no God, but Allah) as the highest, and the word of Kufr (disbelief) as lowest, and this is what Allah tells us in the Qur'an to do. So it is a compulsory duty upon all the Muslims around the world to join the Jihad, although many of them are misguided and Allah did not choose them…[100]"*. In the South African case, the power of IS social media is also reinforced by radical clerics on the ground working with disaffected youth[101].

The power of IS social media was also evident in Nigeria where 24,000 young people were stopped from leaving the country by authorities between January 2014 and March 2015. The majority of these were stopped from emigrating for fear that they were planning to join IS[102]. Authorities account for the increase of IS recruits from Nigeria as a result of a combination of three factors, high youth unemployment, the alliance between Boko Haram and IS as well as the power of social media. Over and above the recruitment videos they put out, IS has also developed close ties with Nigerian criminal syndicates to arrange travel documents, visas, air tickets and money for their recruits[103]. In addition, IS has assisted would-be recruits with sophisticated routes to reach them to hide their end destination from authorities. In August 2015, for instance, India arrested two Nigerian students who were attempting to cross into Pakistan and to eventually find their way to Iraq to join with IS[104]. In the Nigerian case, then, Islamic State did not only actively recruit from Nigeria via social media, but also assisted would-be recruits to get to IS-controlled territory in the Middle East.

Exposure to IS social media played a key role in radicalization of 23 year-old Tunisian engineering student SeifeddineRezgui. Rezgui. He was a Real Madrid soccer fan and participated in break-dance competitions and rap music[105]. Yet within a few months of reading IS posts on social media, Rezgui, also known by the IS *nom de guerre* of Abu Yahya al Qayrawni, would kill 38 foreign tourists on a beach resort in Sousse with an AK-47[106]. His last two postings on Facebook were indeed ominous. In the one he wrote, "*If jihad is a crime, the world shall know that I'm a criminal*"[107]. In the other the desperation and hopelessness in his tone is all too apparent, "*May God take me out of this unjust world and perish its people and make them suffer. They just remember you when you die*"[108]. These words also remind us of the high youth unemployment in Tunisia. It was this same impoverishment and hopelessness which resulted in the self-immolation of a young street vendor in SidiBouzeid in Tunisia which ignited what came to be known as the Arab Spring[109]. There seems to be a definite correlation between poverty and radicalization[110]. One survey conducted just after the Bardo attack in Tunisia's poorest region – the north-west – revealed that over half of the region's youth were willing to join IS[111]. These structural conditions also, then, served to make Rezgui more susceptible to radicalization stemming from IS social media outlets.

Similarly, in June 2015, a 17-year-old Briton – TalhaAsmal - enjoyed the dubious reputation of being that country's youngest suicide bomber when he detonated his SUV packed with explosives in Baiji – a northern Iraqi town[112]. A week later, it emerged that three British sisters together with their nine children left the country to join their brother also in Syria with IS. In the case of both Asmal and the three sisters what appealed to them was the ideological position of IS communicated via social media to establish an Islamic caliphate as this was "… *laid out in sharia law, as a precursor to the Islamic Armageddon enshrined in Hadith literature, based on Prophet Mohammed's prophecy*"[113].

In addition to using such social media platforms, Islamic State is also quite adept at hacking their adversaries Twitter accounts. On 12 January 2015, for instance, IS hacked into and took control of the United States military's Central Command's (CENTCOM) Twitter and YouTube accounts[114]. The IS member who undertook this operation was Junaid Hussain, a 21-year-old hacker from Birmingham, England who was a prominent member of the CyberCaliphate, an IS unit charged with conducting cyber warfare[115]. Whilst the Pentagon was quick to announce that this breach in their cyber-security did not compromise the security of sensitive documents, it was clearly an embarrassment to Washington and clearly a political coup for IS and their supporters which no doubt would add further recruits to their ranks. The Cyber Caliphate also deploys sophisticated encryption methods to avoid detection[116].

Running a sophisticated social media programme, engaging in various social projects focusing on community upliftment (deploying softer power) needs financial resources. So how is Islamic State funded?

Economic Instruments: Funding Islamic State

With 6 out of 10 oil fields in Syria and other such oil fields in Iraq, under its control, Islamic State is in possession of a vast war chest – estimated at US$ 2 billion[117]. Moreover, IS makes an estimated US $1 million per day through the sale and control of oil, according to the US Department of the Treasury[118]. Much of this oil finds its way from the Syrian border town of Besaslan into Hatay, in Turkey – a half-hour drive. In Hatay, oil is a much-prized commodity on account of the high-costs of `black gold' in Turkey – US $7,50 per gallon[119]. Oil, however, has its drawbacks given the falling price of crude on world markets. Oil installations, are also vulnerable to airstrikes.

As such, Islamic State, as any corporation will do in turbulent times is seeking to diversify its portfolio. One such area is narco-trafficking. Currently IS makes US $1 billion per year from Afghan heroin trafficked through the territory it controls. There is also mounting evidence that Islamic State has expanded its drug-trafficking operations in Libya[120]. Libya, and specifically the area that it controls in the coastal region of Sirte is also important for IS since this is the base of their human-trafficking operations into the Mediterranean Sea[121]. Perversely many of those trafficked are refugees fleeing from Syria where IS played a major role in their displacement. Neither does this perversity end here. Having created the conditions of death and destruction in Iraq, the authorities in Baghdad has also documented evidence where Islamic State is playing a major role in organ trafficking[122].

A further US $1 million per day is accrued from extortion and taxation[123]. For instance, pharmacy owners had to pay between US $100 and US $200 per month whilst building contractors had to pay between 5 and 10 percent from every building assignment to the group[124]. The illicit sale of artefacts from Iraq and Syria also add to their financial resources[125]. This can be quite lucrative. In one incident, and from a single dig site, IS made US $ 36 million. Some of these artefacts from this single dig site were over 8,000 years old[126]. The smuggling of raw materials is another source of income[127]. In addition, IS has captured vast sums of money from bank vaults in towns it has captured[128]. When IS took over Mosul, for instance, it looted the central bank and smaller provincial banks securing a financial windfall of hundreds of millions of dollars[129].

Raqqa, the *de* facto IS capital, also happens to be the breadbasket of Syria. Cotton and wheat is produced here and sales of these products find their way once again into the coffers of IS[130]. In Iraq, a similar dynamic is at play. IS-controlled territory in Iraq is where 40 percent of the country's wheat is grown[131]. In addition, kidnapping has proven an equally lucrative enterprise. During 2014, IS was paid US $45 million in ransom payments[132]. Islamic State also receives funds from sympathizers around the world – most notably from such wealthy Gulf States like Qatar and Kuwait[133]. David Cohen, the Under-Secretary for Terrorism and Financial Intelligence at the US Treasury noted that both Qatar and Kuwait remain, "...*permissive jurisdictions for terrorist financing*"[134]. IS has also attracted donors from further afield. Terrorist financing to Islamic State became clear at South Africa's OR Tambo International Airport when five South Africans were apprehended with US $6 million in cash[135]. The men were on their way from Johannesburg to Dubai and the money seized is believed to have been destined for IS[136].

All this provided IS the requisite funds for its operational activities and to develop a patronage network earning them the support of locals. In the process, IS has displaced rivals organizations in a given area. In Mosul and the wider Ninawa Province, the jihadist Jamaat Ansar al-Islam and the Ba'athist Jaysh Rijal al-Tariqat al-Naqshbandia were forced out by IS by essentially buying over local communities[137].

At the same time, the militant group keeps it operational costs low by providing small stipends as opposed to large salaries to its "employees" and looting military equipment and appropriating infrastructure[138]. Ultimately, the deployment of its political and economic instrument is secondary to its military strategy and tactics. Without the successful deployment of force, IS would not be able to take over a given area. Without military victories, Islamic State would be able to galvanize its supporters through social media.

Military Instruments: Strategy and Tactics

Given IS's religious ideology and its desire to create a caliphate based on the 7th century model of governance of the first Islamic state, commentators often view the movement as anachronistic. However, there is nothing anachronistic about IS' military strategy and tactics. Indeed, given the odds stacked against it, the group has displayed tremendous sophistication. One major reason accounting for this sophistication in military prowess is the fact that the upper echelons of the organization are dominated by hardened military professionals – many from Saddam Hussein's armed forces. Al-Baghdadi's chief of the general military council of ISIS was Abu Abdul-Rahman al-Bilawi (real name: Adnan Ismael Najm). He was a captain in Saddam Hussein's army and like Al-Baghdadi was also imprisoned at Camp Bucca. Al-Bilawi was killed in Mosul in June 2014. Another Saddam-era Iraqi officer was Abu Ali al-Anbari. Widely considered as Al-Baghdadi's deputy, he rose up the IS ranks on the basis of his military skills and political pragmatism and not because over his command of Islamic theology. Indeed, even amongst his IS supporters, Al-Anbari's knowledge of Islam is considered rudimentary[139]. Another IS commander is Abu Omar al-Shishani (real name: Tarkhan Batirashvili) who is an ethnic Chechen but who served in the US-trained Georgian army as a military intelligence officer. He fought in the Russo-Georgian War of 2008[140]. As with Al-Anbari, Al-Shishani's knowledge of Islam is practically non-existent. Indeed he is the butt of jokes on various jihadi forums where one noted that Al-Shishani's understanding of Islam is "shit"[141]. Unlike other jihadi organizations, then, one of the key reasons for IS success lay in the fact that senior appointments in Islamic State's military hierarchy is on the basis of military professionalism not religious faith.

Moreover, it is also important to recognize that the group has the dual capabilities to fight both conventional and asymmetric warfare on account of the weapons which is now in its arsenal. These include: 30 Soviet-era T-55 tanks, 10 newer T-72 battle tanks, SA-7 surface-to-air missile systems, BM-21 Grad multiple rocket launchers, Fim-92 Stinger Manpad shoulder-fired infrared homing surface-to-air missiles, ZU-23-2 anti-aircraft guns and M79 Osa, HJ-8 and AT-4 Spigot anti-tank weapons[142]. Often IS would switch from conventional to asymmetric warfare and vice versa, confusing their opponents on the battlefield.

Following IS' loss of Kobane to Kurdish Peshmerga and US-led aerial bombardment and its loss of Tikrit to Iraqi Special Forces (ISF) in April 2015[143], many were already writing the group's obituary. Despite, these setbacks, the group managed a month later, in May 2015, to capture Ramadi, the capital of Iraq's Anbar Province as well as Palmyra in Syria. Commenting on this sudden reversal of fortunes Tim Arango and Anne

Barnard[144] wrote, *"Confounding declarations of the group's decline, the twin offensives have become a sudden showcase for the groups' disciplined adherence to its core philosophies: always fighting on multiple fronts, wielding atrocities to scare off resistance and, especially, enforcing its caliphate in the Sunni heartland that straddles the Iraqi-Syrian border. In doing so, the Islamic State has not only survived setbacks but has also engineered new victories"*.

Again, the choice of cities chosen for the offensive was strategic. Palmyra, despite its relative small geographical size has three main strategic advantages. First, the capture of the town gives IS access to new oil and gas fields. This is especially important given the US aerial attacks on the group's current oil infrastructure. Second, Palmyra sits astride a critical network of roads with which to move ones forces or to supply them. Third, it is an ancient site providing the militants with another lucrative source of revenues – the illicit trafficking of antiquities[145]. Ramadi's strategic significance, meanwhile, lay in the fact that some Sunni tribes not only remained outside of IS but in some cases actively resisted IS' influence over Sunnis[146]. With the capture of Ramadi, IS' control over Iraq's Sunni heartland was now complete. It is also important to understand that there is a close interplay between IS military strategy and the articulation of its political goals. Shortly after the fall of Ramadi, then, IS started to speak on behalf of Sunnis in Iraq, articulating Sunni grievances against the Shia Baghdad government. In the process, this led to its enhanced perceived legitimacy[147] amongst local Sunnis, thereby consolidating its military victory in the area.

From a tactical point of view, the IS strategy to capture Palmyra demonstrated excellent command of psychological warfare. Recognizing that many of Assad's soldiers in the garrison were demoralized, the group decided to add to this by decapitating dozens of soldiers and members of their families and widely disseminated the images[148]. Hardly surprisingly, then, that the garrison at Palmyra did not put up a fight.

The tactical brilliance of IS commanders were on display in the capture of Ramadi. Here IS made use of the elements – in this case, timing their offensive with the appearance of a sandstorm, to ensure maximum confusion amongst the defenders of Ramadi. IS began their attack with 10 massive car bombs – each explosive having similar power to that of the Oklahoma truck bomb two decades ago[149]. These explosions levelled entire city blocks creating mass confusion. At the same time IS sleeper cells in Ramadi started attacking senior officers within the city, thereby decapitating command and control within the armed forces. At this point, the ground offensive started. The remaining Iraqi troops then fled the city. Despite being outnumbered by Iraqi forces, IS' superior tactics won them the city.

In the run-up to the attack on Ramadi, IS also revealed its deep knowledge of the Iraqi armed forces – demonstrating their ability to reconnoiter and gather intelligence on their targets. Recognizing that regular Iraqi forces scarcely provide a challenge to it and recognizing that Iraqi Special Forces (ISF), who were trained and armed by the US, constitutes its real threat, it sought to ensure that the ISF were as dispersed as possible. In the weeks before their major Ramadi offensive, IS deliberately embarked on several minor operations whose aim was to stretch the ISF to the maximum. As a result at the time of the offensive on Ramadi the ISF were dispersed[150] across several theatres and could not respond to the capture of Ramadi. By July 2015, IS forward positions were a mere 65 kilometres from Baghdad[151].

Recognizing how dire the situation actually is for his beleaguered government, Iraqi Prime Minister Haider al-Abadi attempted to recapture Ramadi, the key to the retake of Anbar Province, in August 2015. However, two Iraqi generals – Major-General Abdulrahman Abu Ragheef and Brigadier-General Safeen Abdulmajid - central to the planned offensive were killed by IS. IS made use of captured American Humvees which allowed the suicide bombers driving the explosive-laden vehicles to appear as Iraqi soldiers allowing them to get close to the generals before detonating their lethal cargoes[152]. In addition to respectively killing the Deputy Head of Anbar Operations Command and the head of the Iraqi Army's 10th Division, a number of roadside bombs as well as booby-trapped buildings had resulted in large-scale casualties amongst Iraqi soldiers preparing for the planned offensive. Needless to say, that this has not only sapped morale, but has also resulted in no major offensive on Ramadi[153] in August 2015.

Given the strategic importance of Libya to Europe and Africa, it is important to reflect a bit more on this troubled country and the advances of IS. 20th October 2011 marked the capture and killing of Libyan strongman Colonel Muammar Gaddafi[154]. What followed was a short-lived period of hope as Libyans contemplated democratic reforms following almost 42-years of the iron-fisted authoritarian rule of the colonel and his coterie. Hopes were quickly dashed as the political vacuum was increasingly filled by IS and Islamist-affiliated IS groups have been making in recent months in the country. In July and October 2014 Benghazi and Derna respectively fell under IS control[155]. Since then, IS has expanded the territory under their control in Libya making major advances to the east, south and west of Sirte, including the capture of the Gadabya air base[156]. IS fighters are also making headway towards Misrata on the coastal road to Tripoli. Interestingly enough Islamic State fighters are being quite innovative in tactics using a combination of asymmetric tactics and conventional warfare. Conventional IS forces only advance after individual suicide bombers as well as those in cars detonate their explosives thereby sowing maximum confusion. As IS fighters advance on Misrata suicide bombers wreaked havoc on the city by detonating their bombs. In one such incident on 31 May 2015, five people were killed and a further eight wounded[157] - a clear example of psychological warfare. We have seen these tactics being used more recently in IS advances in Palmyra in Syria and Ramadi in Iraq[158]. The increased sophistication of attacks seems to be related to the influence of Gaddafi's former officers, who alienated from the current *status quo* in which they are marginalized, made common cause with IS[159]. The sophistication of IS military strategy in Libya is also seen in the fact that their targets were specifically chosen such as the Great Man Made River water project – the largest irrigation scheme in the word – which supplies fresh water to Libya's parched cities[160]. Power stations were also targeted.

The IS *modus operandi* is quite clear across North Africa. Exploit existing grievances in a particular area, utilize returning IS fighters to serve as a force multiplier for existing local militias who have pledged allegiance to the group and in order to ensure command and control from IS central send one of the senior IS commanders as the leader of the local franchise. It is this strategy which was used with such devastating results when young militants of the Islamic Youth Shura Council managed to capture Derna in north-eastern Libya[161]. This strategy was also evident in July 2014, as rival groups fought for control of Benghazi in Libya. Ansar al-Sharia's alignment with IS provided decisive. Libyans who fought in Iraq and Syria were then ordered to return to their home country and fight on the side of Ansar al-Sharia. These hundreds of battle-hardened veterans proved decisive in Ansar al-Sharia's capture of several parts of Benghazi[162].

It is important to understand that IS expansion and penetration into regions and countries is not willy-nilly but strategic. Nigeria, for instance, is Africa's most populous country, the biggest economy and a regional hegemon in West Africa. The strategic importance of Nigeria for IS should not be under-estimated. As Peter Pham[163] recently noted about Boko Haram, "*We have a group holding territory and shooting down jet fighters … If Nigeria collapses – it is the strong state in the region – there are no strong states to contain what would happen if Boko Haram succeeds in carving out an Islamic state in that area*".

In similar fashion, Tunisia, too was targeted by IS because according to Larry Diamond[164], it is, "*Alone among the Arab States, it has achieved a remarkable level of political compromise among secular parties and the principal Islamist party, Ennhada*". Indeed, the moderate Islamists of Ennhada has one minister and three junior ministers in the coalition government[165]. The terrorist attack on 18 March 2015 on the Bardo museum in Tunis in which 21 foreign tourists were killed and a further 42 were injured[166] as well as the 26 June 2015 deadly assault on Sousse, a beach resort which resulted in 38 foreign tourists killed[167] then aimed to undermine Tunisia's relative success at forging a democracy with compromises between secularists and moderate Islamists. From this perspective then, the objective of the attacks was to cause greater polarization within society between more liberal-minded and those more religiously-oriented. With more than 3,000 Tunisian trained jihadis having returned to their home country after receiving training in camps in Iraq, Libya and Syria[168], one can expect more attacks in the future.

IS strategy in the West, of course, is different as it cannot control territory in non- Muslim-dominated regions. As such its strategy of terrorism is aimed, as explained earlier, to increase greater polarisation and get the authorities to overreact. The attacks on Paris in January 2015 on a Jewish market and the offices of the Charlie Hebdo magazine, meanwhile, illustrate part of the group's *modus operandi* in Europe. The three perpetrators – brothers Cherif and Said Kouachi[169] and Amedy Coulibaly[170] were well-known to the security forces and had, indeed spent time at Paris' notorious Fleury-Merogis prison together[171] and were under surveillance by French authorities. Knowing this, they simply outlasted the resources and attention span of French intelligence agencies by doing nothing untoward to attract attention. Once sure that surveillance had ended – they struck[172]. This, in turn, raises interesting questions for intelligence services everywhere how does one with limited resources maintain surveillance for months on end on hundreds of targets simultaneously? This is made worse by the budgetary constraints as a result of austerity measures undertaken by various Western governments. Under the circumstances, western security experts have become quite pessimistic regarding their ability to end the tsunami of global jihad. Robert Grenier, a former Central Intelligence Agency (CIA) counter-terrorism expert glumly stated, *"The forces of global jihad which Osama bin Laden did so much to inspire are stronger than ever"*[173]. Equally pessimistic, Andrew Parker, the head of Britain's domestic intelligence service noted than an attack on the United Kingdom was highly likely[174].

The Paris attacks were also interesting from another perspective. It was the first time that Al Qaeda – more specifically the Yemeni-based Al Qaeda in the Arabian Peninsula (AQAP) – and IS worked together in a joint operation. The Kouachi brothers were recruited by AQAP following orders from Al Qaeda's Emir – Ayman al Zawahiri – to strike at the Charlie Hebdo offices[175]. The attack on the Jewish market meanwhile was undertaken by an IS recruit – Amedy Coulibaly. Phone records subsequently revealed that the Kouachi brothers and Coulibaly exchanged scores of phone calls in the run-up to and during the attacks. Could this be the start of further cooperation between IS, Al Qaeda and other radical Islamists? Interesting as such a line of questioning may seem, it appears that this was a once-off given the deep rivalry between IS and Al Qaeda as we will see in subsequent chapters. Rather, the co-operation in Paris seems a direct result of personal ties forged in the French prison amongst the perpetrators of this attack.

The Paris attacks were important for a different reason too. It demonstrated that these radical Islamists could learn from past mistakes and adapt their tactics to new circumstances, in particular out-waiting their respective surveillance details. The November 2015 Paris attacks also displayed increasing sophistication in IS-attacks. Here multiple targets were engaged utilizing a combination of suicide bombers and gunmen spraying bullets. 150 people were killed and hundreds more wounded. The targets chosen included a restaurant, a soccer stadium and nightclub[176]. Whilst seemingly randomly chosen, the very ordinariness of the targets selected was designed to spread terror – the fact that an ordinary Parisian going about his or her ordinary business can be targeted anywhere. The ordinariness of the targets were then designed to instil terror amongst Parisians.

The effective deployment of these political, economic and military instruments account for the ongoing appeal and resilience of Islamic State. This, in turn, raises the question of how to respond to the challenge posed by IS.

3 RESPONDING TO ISLAMIC STATE AND GETTING IT WRONG

Abstract:

Current counter-terrorism strategies to degrade and destroy Islamic State are not working. Part of the problem is political correctness, especially on the part of the Obama Administration which refuses to recognize that these global jihadis' views resonate amongst hundreds of millions of Muslims. As a result, Islamic State is under-estimated. Importantly, there is no quick-fix military solution to the challenged posed by Islamic State such as the decapitation of the leadership and aerial strikes against key Islamic State command and control positions. Moreover countries like Shia Iran whilst fighting Islamic State is also serving to further deteriorate the Sunni-Shia divide in the region which also works in Islamic State's favour since they have cast themselves as the defender of Sunni interests. Moscow's intervention on the part of Damascus and Tehran, meanwhile, would further exacerbate such sectarian tensions.

Keywords: Political correctness, Obama Administration, Iran, Russia

Introduction

Time and time again, politicians in the West have indicated that Islamic State is on the ropes or that it will soon be smashed. Victory was declared when Kobane was taken by Kurdish forces following a US aerial bombardment, only to find that IS had strategically withdrawn its forces to go on to capture Ramadi and Palmyra. Counter-terrorism responses to IS has largely failed on account of four inter-connected reasons. First, effective political responses have been bedeviled by the desire to be politically correct. As such, the nature of IS has been misunderstood and policy responses adopted have proven to be either inadequate or counter-productive. Second, this lack of understanding of IS is also reflected in misguided military measures undertaken such as the decapitation of the leadership of Islamic State. Third, the regional response also serves to play into the hands of IS from Saudi Arabia and Turkey's support to the militants to the military involvement of Iran into Iraq and Syria which has exacerbated Sunni-Shi'a tensions on which IS thrives. The entry of Russia into the fray will further exacerbate these sectarian tensions. Fourth, what is decidedly lacking in terms of a comprehensive approach to the threat posed by IS, is an economic response focusing on adopting measures to squeeze the terrorists' finances.

The Political Response: The Dangers of Political Correctness

Part of the problem dogging an effective response to the spread of Islamic State is the danger of political correctness as expressed in the notion that IS reflects some deviation in major Islamic political thought and that its ideology is therefore anathema to most Muslims. The Obama Administration, Bob Taylor argues, "...*seems to have a rule never to identify Islam with 'terrorism'*"[177]. Such a perspective, of course, is reinforced by clerics and other Muslim bodies denouncing IS[178]. Those arguing that IS some sort of lunatic fringe of Islam however cannot explain why gory IS videos graphically portraying decapitations and the like have attracted so many Muslim followers[179].

Go beyond the superficial denunciation of IS, however, and look closely at its ideology and one cannot but come to the conclusion that Islamic State is a natural outcome of much discourses in political Islam for the past 300 years. As Abdel Bari Atwan has noted, "*IS has not sprung from nowhere. It is the latest evolutionary step in the Salafi-jihadi movement...*"[180]. Indeed, Islamic State justifies each of its actions on the basis of precedents set by Islamic tradition. In justifying declaring its statehood, Uthman bin Abd al-Rahman al-Tamimi, a senior official of IS' Shari'a Committees drew parallels between this and the establishment of the first Islamic state by the Prophet Muhammed in Medina[181]. Similarly when IS detractors' attack the organization for the practice of forcing thousands of Yazidi women into sexual slavery, IS responded in their English-language journal Dabiq, that these Yazidi women were the "spoils of war" and is Islamically permissible. The article in Dabiq went on to quote the Qur'anic chapter "Women" where men were allowed to have up to four wives in marriage as well as those women the "*right hands possess*"[182]. For IS, those words literally translate into "captured in battle"[183]. Professor Ehud Toledano, an expert on slavery in Islam at Tel Aviv University concurs with the IS position,

"They are in full compliance with Koranic understanding … what the Prophet has permitted, Muslims cannot forbid"[184]. In August, 2015 reports surfaced that IS had used chemical weapons, specifically mustard gas against the Kurds. Interestingly, a prominent Saudi Al Qaeda supporting cleric – Nasser bin Hamad al-Fahd - who has since shifted his allegiance to IS - issued a fatwa (religious ruling) on the use of weapons of mass destruction, *"If the infidels can be repelled from the Muslims only using such weapons, their use is permissible, even if you kill them without exception and destroy their tillage and stock"*[185].

Ideologically speaking, how is Islamic State's violent attempts to "purify" Islam different from the Wahhabism in Saudi Arabia which declared even fellow Muslims who did not follow the Wahhabist creed apostates? Is it not contemptible that whilst we decry the decapitations committed by IS, there is no similar outcry in the West against the beheadings committed in Saudi Arabia? Can we see no parallel between IS now and Abd al-Qadir's jihad in North Africa in the 1830s and 1840s who like Al-Baghdadi called himself "Commander of the Faithful"? Similarly in the late 19th century Muhammad Ahmad called himself the Mahdi (Redeemer) and conducted his own jihad in Sudan[186].

Ideologically, too, there is little to separate IS from its Islamist antecedents. Muhammed ibn Abd al-Wahhab (CE 1703-1792) famously declared all those who did not conform to his purist vision of Islam to be apostates and worthy of death[187]. MaulanaAbul Ala-Maududi (CE 1903-1979) the founder of the Jamaat-e-Islami organisation in Pakistan and the ideological father of the Taliban movement in Afghanistan and Pakistan is perhaps the best exemplar on the use of force and coercion to deal with difference. He had this to say, *"…force may be used, in fact should be used to prevent people from doing wrong. Non-Muslim countries and cultures cannot be allowed to practice immoral deeds"*[188].
Can policy-makers not witness the ideology of Wahhab and Maududi when IS beheads Coptic Christians, destroy Muslim Sufi shrines or executes members of the Yazidi community? Similarly, when 24 year-old Mohammed Youssef Abdulazeez killed four US Marines and a US Navy petty officer in Chattanooga on 16th July 2015, in an IS-inspired terrorist act he justified this by quoting various Islamic verses justifying the action. The night before he engaged in his murderous rampage Abdulazeez texted one of the 40 most important sayings of the Prophet Muhammed, *"Whosoever shows enmity to a friend of Mine, I [Allah] will indeed declare war against him"*[189]. In line with the tenets of Islamism outlined above, Abdulazeez rejected the separation between Islam from politics. Again he cited Islamic practice to justify the reason for this, *"So this picture that you have in your mind that the Prophet's companions were people being like priests living in monasteries is not true. All of them [were] leaders of an army at the frontlines … very involved in establishing Islam*

in the world ... Every one of them fought Jihad for the sake of Allah. Every one of them had to make sacrifices in their lives"[190]. Having an Islamic State then is the logical outcome of such thinking.

The global ambitions of IS, meanwhile, also follows a logical trajectory from a previous generation of Islamists. The Egyptian Hassan al Banna (1906-1949), founder and Supreme Guide of the Muslim Brotherhood declared, *"It is the nature of Islam to dominate and not to be dominated, to impose its laws on all nations and to extend its power to the entire planet"*[191]. In similar vein, Maududi declared that, *"Islam does not want to bring about the revolution in one country or a few countries. It wants to spread it to the entire world. Although it is the duty of the Muslim Party to bring this revolution first to its own nation, its ultimate goal is world revolution"*[192].

Islamic State is also quite aware of Islamic tradition and its version of the "End Days" which witnesses the forces of *Al-Masih ad-Dajjal*(literally the `False Messiah' or in Christian terms – the `Anti-Christ') pitted against the forces of the Mahdi which would pave the way for the second coming of Jesus[193].The significance of the territory under IS control and threatened by IS cannot be underestimated. According to Islamic tradition, the *Dajjal* is to appear on the way between Iraq and Syria[194], whilst Jesus is to re-appear to the east of Damascus[195]. Damascus also has great symbolic significance. It was the capital of the first Ummayad Caliphate when Muslim Arab armies overran the Eastern Roman and Sassanid Empires[196].

From various Islamic State statements, then, they believe the End of Days is near and they are preparing for the Mahdi and the final battle between good and evil. It is clear that these views resonate amongst Muslims. According to a 2012 Pew poll, it is apparent that a large number of Muslims across the world believe that the end of days is already here and that they will personally witness the final battle between good and evil. In Afghanistan 83 percent of respondents believe this, the figure for Iraq is 72 percent, Tunisia 67 percent and Malaysia 62 percent[197].Thousands of miles from Raqqa, in the sea-side town of Port Elizabeth in South Africa – a South African imam (priest), Rashid Moosagie moved to IS-ruled Syria together with his wife, sons and daughter. In his last message to the community he served for more than 30 years he passionately argues that the final stand-off between good and evil, between Islam and its enemies will be taking place in Syria[198]. Motivated by similar considerations, 25 year-old Nazir Nortei Alema left his native Osu neighborhood in Accra, Ghana to join up with IS to fight the `forces of evil' opposing the 'pure' Islamic state which, in his view, Islamic State represents[199].

This preparation for a Muslim Armageddon is clearly illustrated in a 32-page IS document found in August 2015 in Pakistan entitled *A Brief History of the Islamic State Caliphate*. Journalists have labelled the document akin to Adolf Hitler's *Mein Kampf* (My Struggle)[200]. As with *Mein Kampf* and documents emanating from other militant Islamist movements like Hezbollah, Hamas and Al Qaeda, the document refers to Jewish control of the world where even US President Barack Obama is maligned as *"the Mule of the Jews"*. In the document, IS refers to six phases of their operations which aims to bring about the end of the world. Phase 6 runs from 2017 to 2020 where open warfare, including an apocalyptic confrontation with America will begin. In addition, their plan is also to conquer Rome by 2020. This conquest of Rome is in line with Islamic prophesy that before the Muslim messiah – the Mahdi - appears that two great Roman cities must be conquered. The first was Constantinople which became a Muslim city – Istanbul. Rome then is next on the agenda[201]. Before one ridicules this notion of how terrorists can capture a city of 3 million people in a country of 60 million, it should be borne in mind that IS refers to its sleeper cells in Rome and the support it receives from European Muslims and non-Muslim sympathizers. Consider too that they have entrenched themselves just across the Mediterranean Sea in North Africa[202]. The tone of *A Brief History of the Islamic State Caliphate* is uncompromising, *"Accept the fact that is caliphate will survive and prosper until it takes over the entire world and beheads every last person that rebels against Allah. This is the bitter truth; swallow it"*[203]. As with Hitler's Final Solution, then, all enemies of the caliphate would lose their heads by 2020. It is a scenario where Hitler merges with Robespierre in order for a Muslim nirvana to occur.

The point being made here is a simple one: Islamic State is a logical product of Islamic history – not some deviant new creed which unfathomably emerged on the Islamic landscape. Saladdin Ahmed[204] also underlined this truism, *"The discourse of the complete rejection of the Other has a long history in both Islamism and Arab nationalism ..."* In similar vein, viewing IS as an aberration is extremely problematic given the support their views have amongst large sections of Muslims. Believing such a fairy-tale as the Obama White House would have us believe, obfuscates reality and serves to undermine any serious counter-terrorism effort by drawing a false dichotomy between mainstream Islam and the purported aberration which is Islamic State. In the process, intelligence agencies are blind-sided from the real trajectories of radicalization.

By way of example, consider the following: a rigorous survey conducted by the University of Maryland and World Public Opinion; for instance, found that 76 percent of Moroccan Muslims and 74 percent of Egyptian Muslims wanted the strict application of shar'ia law in every Islamic country. Further, the survey revealed that 71 percent of Moroccans and 67 percent of Egyptians desired this outcome: *"To unify all Islamic countries into a single Islamic state or Caliphate"*[205]. Should we then be surprised when a YouTube video surfaces of a football match in Morocco where fans of the Casablanca club – Raja Club Athletic – chant *"Daesh, Daesh"* (the Arabic acronym for IS) and *"God is Great, let's go on jihad"*. Should we be surprised that an estimated 1500 Moroccans have joined IS?[206]

Further credence to suggest that Islamic State is not merely some sort of lunatic fringe in the Muslim world was a poll conducted by the Qatar-based Al-Jazeera network amongst its Arabic-language viewers. Of the 56,881 polled, a staggering 81 percent voted 'yes' to the question: *"Do you support the victories of the Islamic State in Iraq and Syria (IS) in your region?"*[207] Indeed a survey by the Qatari-based Arab Centre for Research and Policy studies have highlighted the fact that those Muslims who find IS appealing are drawn to its military achievements, its commitment to Islamic principles, its declaration of an Islamic Caliphate and its willingness to stand up to the West[208]. A COMRES Research Institute poll conducted amongst British Muslims, meanwhile, found that 27 percent were sympathetic towards the motives behind the attack on the Charlie Hebdo offices[209]. To put it differently, one in four British Muslims felt that a person insulting the Prophet Muhammed deserved death. Exhaustive surveys conducted by Pew and European Social Survey covering 42 percent of the global Muslim population reveal that 17.38 percent of Muslims worldwide express terror sympathies. To put it differently, almost one in five Muslims or 295 million people globally are potential recruits to IS[210]. Polls such as these also underscore why Muslims in ninety countries have flocked to fight under the IS banner. These surveys also illustrate why it is factually incorrect to think of IS as something marginal or alien to Muslim society as the Obama Administration repeatedly does.

These polls increasingly render hollow declarations from US Presidents and Muslim ulema (clergy) and leaders that *"Islam is a religion of peace"*[211]. As Tarek Fatah[212] has noted, *"It is true that for many Muslims, Islam is a moral compass that guides them in their daily, law-abiding lives. But, for many others, Islam is intrinsically interwoven with the doctrine of armed jihad and the goal of ultimate Muslim supremacy over non-Muslims"*. From a strategic perspective denying the popularity of Islamic State is erroneous in the extreme. How else can one explain the fact that an estimate 31,500 IS fighters[213] can control a population of 10 million in the area they control in Iraq and Syria? Whilst, it may not be politically correct to state it, the simple fact is that there are large numbers of Muslims who in the words of Saladdin Ahmed[214], *"… not only excuse murder, torture, rape, sexual enslavement, and genocide against minorities, but also consider them religious duties".*

Given these developments it is erroneous to view the war against IS in terms of merely seizing this or that town as when Kobane had fallen following sustained United States-led coalition airstrikes followed by a ground offensive of Kurdish Peshmerga troops – or indeed the reported wounding of Al-Baghdadi in an aerial strike. This is first and foremost an ideological struggle between liberal democracies and radical Islamists and will continue long after Kobane or Raqqa changes hands for the umpteenth time and will continue even after the death of an Al-Baghdadi. The West needs to prepare its citizens for a generational struggle.

The problem with much counter-terrorism discourses is that it approaches its subject matter ahistorically. Viewed in a historical context, one can see IS as the logical outgrowth of trends in political Islam which has been with us for the past three centuries. Worse, counter-terrorism discourses imbued with the desire to be politically correct and not to offend misreads IS completely. In the process, strategies against IS prove ineffective at best, counterproductive at worst. The conclusion is a simple one: expect the cancer that is Islamic State to spread and intensify in the coming years.

The Military Response: Decapitating the leadership of Islamic State

Writing in The Spectator, Douglas Murray[215] argues that the Obama White House could be more aggressive in responding to IS by "smashing" the group by dispatching US Special Forces to decapitate the leadership of the movement thereby rendering the movement leaderless. Such a perspective that the fight against IS can be won so easily is however infantile if one considers the structure of IS as discussed in Chapter 1. Indeed the various IS "governance" structures has prompted prominent IS expert, Aymenn Jawad Al-Tamimi[216] to conclude that the organization was "...*sustainable and resistant to internal collapse*". Moreover, succession is built into the organization. When Al-Baghdadi was severely wounded in a US air strike whilst traveling in a three-car convey in Nineveh, Iraq in March 2015, the group immediately announced that Emir Abu Alaa al-Afri would succeed him as interim leader[217]. In other words, then Islamic State is like a hydra – cutting off one head results in the emergence of several other heads.

It is questionable whether such a strategy of decapitation of the leadership will work for other reasons too. Whilst there is effective command and control on the one hand, Islamic State is far from a centralized organization with local commanders having considerable room for independent action.

Thus, decapitation of senior leaders may well leave local franchises or regional commands unaffected. Despite this, the decapitation of the leaders of militant groups seems to be the preferred method embarked upon by the Obama Administration[218]. In June 2015, for instance, the leader of the Al Qaeda in the Arabian Peninsula (AQAP) and the number two within Al Qaeda global – Nasser al-Wuhayshi - was killed in a US drone strike. Whilst his death was hailed by Ned Price, spokesperson of the US National Security Council (NSC) as a "major blow" to Al Qaeda[219], senior Al Qaeda operative Khaled Batarfi declared, *"Let it be known to the enemies of God that their battle is not only with one person or figure, no matter how important"*[220]. As if to emphasize Batarfi's statement, AQAP immediately announced that its military commander – Qassim al-Raymi – will succeed Al-Wuhayshi[221]. It should also be noted that when Anwar al-Awlaki, another senior AQAP operative was killed in an earlier drone strike it made little difference to the lethality of AQAP and the pace of its deadly operations[222]. In fact, AQAP in Yemen has grown stronger throughout 2015. In similar fashion, the US Drug Enforcement Agency (DEA) went after Pablo Escobar, the head of the Medallin drug cartel[223]. His imprisonment however did little to staunch the flow of narcotics from Mexico into the United States. Indeed, his cartel was merely replaced by a far more sophisticated and brutal one – the Zeitas[224].

In August 2015, a senior deputy to IS leader Al-Baghdadi, Fadhil Ahmad al-Hayali, aka Hajji Mutazz, was killed in a US airstrike near Mosul[225]. Whilst the Americans hailed his death as a major blow to the organization citing the fact that he was the movement's Emir of Ninawa Province, that he was the primary coordinator for moving explosives, weapons, troops and vehicles between Iraq and Syria and that his influence within IS spanned the areas of finance, media, operations and logistics. Whilst his death might inconvenience IS for a short time, it is important to bear in mind that previous deputies to Al Baghdadi have been killed before including the IS Emir responsible for military operations in North Africa as well as its "Emir of Oil and Gas". These were however quickly replaced. As one counter-terrorism official opined, *"…Islamic State had created an organic structure that inures it to the death of any single leader"*[226]. In September 2015, the Pentagon-supported and non-partisan think tank, the Rand Corporation reach similar conclusions: *'The coalition has successfully targeted numerous senior leaders, but the organization's [IS] focus on creating a deep bench of personnel means that attacking individual leaders will not destroy the group. Replacements will rise, and any damaging effect will be temporary"*[227]. The point being simply made is that the fight against IS will not be quick and no amount of the decapitation of the leadership of IS by itself will render the movement "smashed".

The Military Response: Aerial Strikes vs Boots on the Ground

There are, however, other questions relating to the US approach towards IS. Whilst US President Obama's stated goal is to *"degrade and ultimately destroy"* the militant grouping, the reality is that this cannot be accomplished from the air[228]. Between September 2014 and June 2015, there were nearly 4000 airstrikes on IS positions by the American-led coalition. The airstrikes however were compromised by the political objectives set by Washington. For instance, airstrikes were not launched if the Assad regime could benefit from it and retake territory captured by IS. Whilst, understandable, in practice its means, according to Aymenn Jawad al-Tamimi[229] that large swathes of territory controlled by IS in central and south-eastern Syria have remained unscathed from the airstrikes. Senator John McCain, who chairs the US Senate Armed Services Committee is also dismissive on the effectiveness of US-led aerial strikes. He pointed out in July 2015 that 75 percent of coalition planes were returning to their bases without using any of their munitions. The reason for this would appear to be that there were no forward air controllers on the ground to provide the airplanes with details on the targets[230].

The Pentagon, however, disagrees with this gloomy assessment on the effectiveness of airstrikes. According to the Pentagon, these airstrikes led to the deaths of 10,000 IS militants[231]. Even if one accepts these figures from the US Department of Defense, the sad reality is that IS continues to attract ever more recruits and continue to capture territory and spread its tentacles far beyond Iraq and Syria. In other words, any state no matter how fragile or provisional cannot be destroyed with an aerial campaign alone. Ultimately, ground forces will have to be inserted on recaptured IS territory to prevent it from being infiltrated once again by IS fighters. The Obama Administration, however, is adamant that there will be no US troops placed in a combat role in either Iraq or Syria. This is understandable in a democracy. A CNN poll demonstrated that 61 percent of American public opinion was opposed to US soldiers engaged in combat missions against IS in Iraq and Syria[232]. Respecting the popular will of one's citizens however does not necessarily make strategic sense.

Despite the reluctance on the part of the Obama Administration to put US boots on the ground, in October 2015 the US agreed to deploy no more than 50 Special Forces commandos. The Pentagon made clear that these would serve as forward air controllers to provide details of IS targets to coalition airplanes as well as to train and advise the Syrian moderate rebels. Washington, however, was adamant that these commandos did not constitute 'boots-on-the-ground' since they were assigned non-combative roles[233]. Current US policy, then, begs the question of who these ground forces will be given the US reluctance to place 'boots on the ground'?

Whilst the US initially spoke about training and arming the so-called moderate opposition forces in Syria and Iraq, the figures of those having received such training in Iraq by June 2015 is a pitiful 60 and for Syria a mere 90[234]. Four months later, in October 2015, a senior US military commander informed the US Congress that only 4 or 5 of these Syrian fighters were effectively engaged in the fight against IS. Since July 2014, US $500 million was spent training moderate Syrian rebels and more than a year later, one has only a maximum of five fighters on the ground taking on Islamic State[235]. Granted, recruitment is bogged down by a number of factors including vetting potential recruits to ensure that they are not playing for the other side. Still, at this rate by the time there are sufficient numbers of trained recruits IS would have long captured Damascus and Baghdad.

Moreover, the US position that the Syrian rebels they train should not attack the Assad regime and only take on IS further compounds the problem for the Americans. Having been on the receiving end of Assad's draconian rule, including Assad's forces indiscriminate use of barrel bombs against hapless civilians, Syrian rebels are understandably unhappy with Washington's position of not attacking Assad' forces[236]. This was a breath-taxingly naïve position on the part of the Obama Administration – to militarily train and supply Syrian rebels and insist that they do not attack the regime which has brutalized them!. In addition, the costs for training each recruit is prohibitively high – at an estimated US $4 million for each recruit[237]. To compound matters still further, the first 50 recruits who were trained in Turkey, crossed the border into Syria and essentially went missing – no contact could be established with these recently trained recruits![238] Another US-trained recruit, AnasObaid, who was a senior rebel commander, meanwhile, defected to Al Qaeda-aligned Jabhat al-Nusra – handing them also an arsenal of US-supplied weapons[239].

The Regional Response: The Achilles' Heel of the US-led coalition against IS: Saudi Arabia and Turkey

One cannot but come to the conclusion that the current US-strategy towards ISis bound to fail. Indeed, so desperate is Washington to claim some success that the US Defense Department's Inspector-General has launched an investigation into whether senior US military officials have "*...skewed intelligence assessments to present a more optimistic picture*"[240]. One reason accounting for this failure relates to who the US' allies are in this grand coalition against IS. In September 2014, on the 13th anniversary of 9/11, US Secretary of State John Kerry met with the leaders of 10 Arab states in Jeddah, Saudi Arabia as Washington sought to build their coalition against IS[241]. However the irony of this is clearly evident in the fact that Saudi Arabia and Qatar together with billionaires in the other Gulf Arab states have been supporting radical Islamism for decades. Indeed Tarek Fatah[242] cogently emphasizes the point that, *"Islamic State is being formed exactly the way Saudi Arabia was formed when thousands of bloodthirsty jihadis rose from the Sultanate of Nejd and invaded the Kingdom of Hejaz, slaughtering the country's citizens into submission in 1925".* Saudi Arabia has spent more than US $100 billion to spread Wahhabism across the world. This, Wahhabism, according to Tarek Fatah[243] is *"...the foundational creed of IS, the Muslim Brotherhood, al-Qaeda, Boko Haram and the Taliban".* In 2002, Laurent Murawiec, a geostrategist at the Rand Corporation warned the US Department of Defense that the, *"Saudis are very active at every level of the terrorist chain, from planners to financiers, from cadre to foot soldier, from ideologist to cheerleader ... Saudi Arabia supports our enemies and attacks our allies"*[244]. Under the circumstances, one should not be surprised that the largest contingent of foreign fighters in IS ranks are Saudis. According to Fernando Betancor[245] there are 7,000 Saudi nationals amongst IS fighters.

Similarly, Alistair Crooke a former British MI-6 agent bluntly opined, *"You can't understand IS if you don't know the history of Wahhabism in Saudi Arabia"*[246]. Under the circumstances, it is any wonder that the overwhelming number of IS Twitter users are located in Saudi Arabia, almost double the number of Syria, where the IS "capital" of Raqqa is located[247]. Neither should this surprise one. Despite the condemnations against IS emanating from Riyadh and other Gulf Co-operation Council (GCC) capitals, the reality is that there is considerable support for IS in these states[248]. This was once again highlighted in October 2015 when Saudi Prince Abd al-Muhsen bin Walid al-Aziz Al Saud was arrested just as his private jet was about to depart from Beirut's Rafik Hariri International Airport. He was in possession of two tons of the narcotic Captogon. Captogon is an amphetamine-based drug which Islamic State fighters use to stay alert whilst in battle. It produces a kind of euphoria, keeping sleep and tiredness at bay whilst giving IS fighters greater energy. The Centre Star which broke the story is adamant that these drugs were being smuggled to Islamic State[249].

Moreover, it is imperative to underline that the war against Islamic State is ultimately an ideological struggle between liberal democracies and the neo-fascists which is Islamic State. The various polls discussed earlier in this study underline this fact. If this is indeed, the case why is it that the US' allies happen to have the same ideological underpinnings as does IS? Is it a co-incidence that there were more beheadings in Saudi Arabia for the first six months of 2015 than in the areas IS controlled? From the beginning of January 2015 to the first week of June 2015, Saudi Arabia beheaded 100 individuals[250]. Indeed, the demand is so great that this Wahhabist Kingdom had to recruit additional executioners in 2015. Moreover, whilst we may be appalled by the human rights violations of IS, for instance, its treatment of women, we should also recall that Saudi Arabian King Abdullah had his own daughters imprisoned to compel their mother to return after she fled from him[251]. The real rivalry between Riyadh and Raqqa is not an ideological one but who gets to lead 1.5 billion Muslims. The Saudi King who has the title of Custodian of the Two Holy Mosques or the Caliph of IS?[252]From a strategic perspective, too, Sunni Islamic State poses a far bigger threat to Shi'a Iran than Sunni Saudi Arabia. Thus the Saudi Kingdom despite signing up for the US coalition may not want to see the radicals defeated given the ongoing rivalry between Riyadh and Tehran.

Another key ally in the anti-IS US coalition and who happens to be a North Atlantic Treaty Organization (NATO) member is Turkey. Like Saudi Arabia, Turkey under the increasingly Islamist Recep Erdogan is also a flawed ally. Turkey boasts the dubious reputation of having jailed the most number of journalists in the world. Under Erdogan, Turkish secularism has increasingly come under threat[253]. Moreover, this key US ally in the war against IS also happens to be one of the biggest sources of IS recruits![254]Lik e Saudi Arabia, Turkey too has a vested interest in supporting IS. Ultimately, Turkey believes that only IS can defeat the Assad regime in Syria and Rojava, the emerging Kurdish state in the north-east which is aligned with Turkey's own restive Kurds in the form of the Kurdistan Workers' Party (PKK)[255]. It is interesting too that IS targets on Turkish soil just happened to be foes of Recep Erdogan. Consider for instance the repeated targeting by IS of the pro-Kurdish Peoples' Democratic Party (HDP) as well as the bombing of a pro-Kurdish gathering in August 2015 as well as the 10 October 2015 Turkish-Kurdish peace march. The latter bombing resulted in 105 marchers killed and over 400 injured[256]. It was political activism on the part of the HDP which prevented Erdogan in the 7 June 2015 elections from introducing an executive presidential system[257]. BurakBekdil[258] also points out that another group ideologically and politically opposed to Erdogan's increasingly draconian rule, the Alevis in Turkey have also borne the brunt of IS attacks.

Given these developments, the opposition HDP filed a motion in parliament calling for an investigation into the activities of IS inside Turkey. However the motion was defeated by members of Erdogan's ruling party[259]. Perhaps, it is understandable why the government is opposed to any independent enquiry given their purported collusion with IS. Evidence of this collusion came to light in July 2015 when two Chechen jihadists who were part of an IS cell – Magomet Abdurakmanov and Ahmad Ramzanov – were captured in Istanbul. In his trial Abdurakmanov told the court, *"We were in contact with Turkish intelligence all the time. Turkey sent us arms, cars and money when we were fighting in Syria. Turkey was helping us because we were fighting against [Syrian President] Bashar al-Assad"*[260]. Further evidence of collusion soon appeared when a Turkish nurse revealed details of the activities of President Erdogan's daughter, Sumeyye Erdogan, in providing medical care to injured Islamic State militants brought to Turkish hospitals in Sanliurfa[261].

Whilst ostensibly part of the US-led campaign to degrade and destroy IS, for instance, by engaging in airstrikes against IS targets in Syria, Turkey is playing a double role. The majority of these Turkish airstrikes seems to be directed at Kurdish targets as opposed to IS[262]. Similarly, the Turkish position of creating a so-called "safe-zone" to the north of Aleppo is directed less at IS and more at Kurdish forces. The aim of such a "safe-zone" is to prevent Syrian Kurdish Protection Units (YPG) from linking up with Turkish Kurdish militants in the Turkish canton of Afrin[263]. In addition, Turkey has done little to end the movement of jihadis across Turkey's borders into Syria. Indeed, beyond turning a blind eye to this jihadi highway, Turkish intelligence services have actively assisted such crossings[264].
Turkey's active support for IS, according to Daniel Pipes is manifested in a number of ways:

- Ankara has paid US $800 million to IS for oil shipments
- Active duty Turkish soldiers have been training IS members
- Turkish Prime Minister Recep Erdogan has met three times with Yasin al-Qadi who has close ties to IS and has funded it
- Turkey has provided the bulk of IS' funds, logistics, training and arms to IS
- Turkish ambulances cross into Syria and evacuate IS casualties to Turkish hospitals. One such case was a photograph which surfaced showing a senior IS Commander Abu Mohammed in a Hatay State Hospital receiving treatment for battle wounds[265].

With friends like these, the saying goes, who needs enemies? Can Washington not see the obvious contradiction in having such allies to defeat IS? Moreover, in an ideological struggle between liberal democracy and the neo-Fascist Islamism of IS, how does one justify one's allies having similar views to those of IS? Under the circumstances, it is perhaps understandable that President Obama recently admitted that his administration does not have a "complete strategy" to defeat IS![266]

The Regional Response: Sectarian strife, the Rise of Iran and the Dismemberment of States

Washington's reluctance, to put boots on the ground has resulted in it relying on local actors such as the Iraqi army and the Kurdish Peshmerga. Clearly the latter has proven their worth in the battle for Kobane where US aerial power and Peshmerga forces worked together to oust IS from the city. The Iraqi troops however are far more unreliable with them having fled in several instances, leaving their weapons behind, for instance in Ramadi, even when they outnumbered IS fighters. More problematic, is that when they have captured cities from IS – it was with Shia militias who have engaged in revenge killings against Sunni residents thereby exacerbating the sectarian divide in the country[267].

As Jonathan Spyer[268] has demonstrated three of the four largest Shi'a formations in Iraq – the Badr Organization, the Kata'ibHizballah[269] and Asaibahlal-Haq – are directly affiliated to Tehran. The fourth – Moqtada al Sadr's Saraya al-Salam militia is more autonomous but remains pro-Iranian. Moreover, these Shia militias often operate under the command of the Iranian Revolutionary Guard Corps (IRGC) and indeed IRGC personnel and its Quds force have actively participated in the fighting. Quds force teams are already located in Samarra, Baghdad, Karbala and Tikrit[270]. Whilst, Iran often argues that it is only involved in an advisory capacity in Syria, their force deployment certainly contradicts their official position. The fact that Iranian forces are involved in frontline fighting was also evident when a senior Iranian Revolutionary Guard commander, General Hossein Hamedani, was killed in fighting in Aleppo[271]. Under the circumstances, Jonathan Spyer's[272] conclusion is sobering:

"An Iranian stealth takeover of Iraq is currently under way. Tehran's actions in Iraq lay bare the nature of Iranian regional strategy. They show that Iran has no peers at present in the promotion of a very 21st century of war, which combines the recruitment and manipulation of sectarian loyalties; the establishment and patient sponsoring of political and paramilitary front groups; and the engagement of these groups in irregular and clandestine warfare, all in tune with an Iran-led agenda".

The Iranian presence and Shi'a militias together with the Iraqi army also works to support IS. Mohamed al-Dulaimi, a resident of IS-controlled Fallujah was asked by a journalist what will happen if Shi'a militias entered the city. His response was unequivocal, *"We will take our guns and fight them, not because we are IS, but because the militias will kill us all"*[273]. The current US strategy is not only making IS stronger, but also strengthening the hand of Iran which the 2015 annual report on terrorism published by the US State Department unequivocally states is still continuing its "terrorist-related" activity[274].

A similar dynamic is working in Syria where Shi'a Iran is supporting the ruling Alawite minority led by Assad. The Alawite, incidentally, is a cultural off-shoot of the Shi'a[275]. Understandably, Sunnis in the Middle East speak of the creeping Shi'a Crescent. The involvement of Iran and its proxies has changed the military balance in some fundamental ways in favour of the Asad regime. The Syrian Army together with the pro-Iranian Hezbollah having captured the Qalamoun Mountains[276] has effectively resulted in one group of Sunni terrorists – IS – having been replaced by Shi'a terrorists – Hezbollah. In the process, this has effectively strengthened two terrorist states – Tehran and Damascus[277].

It is however not only Iraqi Shia militia who Iranian forces are working with but also the Kurdish Peshmerga. Tehran, for instance, has already deployed 7 SU-25 ground attack aircraft to support Kurdish and Iraqi ground offensives[278]. This raises a perverse scenario where US aerial bombardments of IS creates the space for the expansion of Iran into Iraq – exactly what happened with the US invasion of Iraq in 2003 where the ouster of Saddam Hussein resulted in the expansion of Iranian influence into Iraq. To put it differently, in an effort to remove Sunni Islamist extremism in the form of IS, the US aerial strikes are creating the conditions for the spread of Shia Islamist extremism in the form of Iran – a state sponsor of terrorism[279].

The issue of the need for ground forces to take the fight to IS (without benefiting Iran) still however remains. This conundrum is further aggravated by the fact that both the Iraqi forces and the Peshmerga made clear that whilst they will fight IS in Iraq, they will not cross the border into Syria to take the fight to IS there despite the Islamic State's *de facto* capital is in Raqqa in Syria[280]. So who would constitute the ground forces in Syria? One answer which springs to mind is the Syrian rebels opposed to the Assad regime. However, Jonathan Spyer reminds us that these, "...*Syrian rebels are characterized by extreme disunity, questionable effectiveness, and the presence of hardline Sunni Islamists elements among their most committed units*"[281]. Indeed, the most effective of organizations amongst the Syrian rebel ranks is Jabhat al-Nusra which is allied to Al Qaeda[282]. From a policy perspective, the choices on offer is equally bad. On the one hand, there is IS or Al Qaeda in the driver's seat in Syria. Alternatively the Iranian-backed Assad regime together with Iranian proxies like Hezbollah declare victory. Under the circumstances, the Obama administration is increasingly moving away from its stated goal of the destruction of IS and is increasingly coming to terms with the existence of IS. In September 2014, the White House Chief of Staff Dennis McDonough redefined what success would entail for US policy with regards to IS. This, he declared is when the militant group, "….*no longer threatens our friends in the region, no longer threatens the United States*"[283]. The 3 May 2015 attack on a Prophet Muhammed cartoon contest in Garland, Texas[284] however demonstrates that the White House is deluded to believe that IS can be contained or degraded but not destroyed. Frankly, there may be no option other than US/NATO 'boots on the ground'[285] in the form of Special Forces and bolstering a Sunni force from neighboring countries. The pressing need for an increased coalition military presence on the ground was underlined in April 2015 when the US State Department declared that IS was "*…a significant threat to all our partners in the region and a significant threat to the US homeland. We've never seen something like this. This is a formidable, enormous threat*"[286]. The different statements emanating from the White House and the US State Department, however, also suggest that there are different assessments within the Obama Administration as to the threat posed by IS as well as what to do to eradicate that threat.

The US-crafted strategy (as incomplete as it is) is also problematic in terms of the political objective – maintaining the territorial integrity of Iraq and Syria. The Sunnis in Syria have had enough of the domination of the Alawites of the Assad family. The Sunnis in Iraq meanwhile have similar misgivings with the domination of the Shias and the creeping influence of Shia Iran over Baghdad[287]. Indeed, the fact that Iraqi Shia militia are commanded in battle by Iranian Revolutionary Guards generals and that these have been responsible for human rights violations of Sunnis have not gone unnoticed. Amnesty International and Human Rights Watch has meticulously documented evidence of Shi'a militias looting Sunni homes and mistreating civilians in Baghdad, Samarra, and Kirkuk[288]. Small wonder then that Hamed al-Mutlaq, a Sunni Member of the Iraqi Parliament declared that, "*The militias are no different from IS*"[289]. Whilst it is common knowledge that IS will not be defeated unless one can pry Sunni tribesmen from the grip of IS, the Americans are providing no incentive to them by leveraging their influence on the authorities in Baghdad to adopt a more inclusive and less sectarian approach to nation-building. As Osama Nujaifi[290], a Sunni and Vice-President of Iraq forcefully asserted, "*We need assurances that those who are fighting against Daesh [the Arabic name for IS] will have rights and be treated like Iraqis*".

The Sunnis tribesmen remember well that in 2006 they fought IS' predecessor – Al Qaeda in Iraq. Sunni Awakening Councils supported US General David Petraeus' offensive against the Islamist militants only to be left to the mercies of the Shia-dominated government in Baghdad[291]. What is clear is that Washington has lost influence over the Baghdad government as Iranian influence over Iraq continues to mount. Whilst Washington has urged Baghdad to arm Sunnis to fight IS, this has not occurred as a result of hard-line Shi'a objections. Indeed, Baghdad is making no attempt to run Iraq along non-sectarian lines. Those Sunni fighters still on the payroll of the Awakening Councils (as of June 2015) have not received a salary in 15 months[292]. Understandably, there is no desire on their part to fight for the Shi'a in Baghdad nor their Iranian backers.

The same could be said about the Kurds. The Kurdish Peshmerga militias have been at the forefront of the war against IS and having liberated places like Kobane and Sinjar[293] on their own with no support from Baghdad, have no desire to be part of a united Iraq. Indeed, at a recent meeting in Washington, D.C in early 2015, President Masoud Barzani of Iraqi Kurdistan publicly stated that the Kurds are moving towards full independence[294]. The bottom-line is this: Washington needs to accept that Iraq will most likely split into three states: Shi'a, Sunni and Kurd. Given the sectarian tensions at play in Syria as well, this country too will be dismembered. The military strategy adopted, then, needs to conform to these new political realities. As Alon Ben-Meir[295] has so cogently argued, *"One of the main pre-requisites to defeating IS in Iraq is to determine the political future of Sunni Iraqis. As long as they do not know what the future has in store for them, they have no reason to put their mind and soul into the fight against IS. The Sunnis are not prepared to make all the needed sacrifices only to benefit the Shiite government in Baghdad, which they reject and despise even more than IS. The Obama administration must begin, concurrently with the fight against IS, to negotiate the future status of the Sunni Iraqis".*

The Sunni-Shi'a divide is also negatively impacting on international diplomatic efforts for a solution. Consider here the case of Syria. Tehran – the main supporter of the besieged Assad regime proposed a plan under which the Syrian government maintains control over its current areas (Damascus, Syrian-Lebanese border, Qalamount, western Ghouta, Zabadani and the western Syrian coast, including Tartus Port). The (non-IS) rebels will maintain control over the areas they currently have. Both regime and rebels will then turn their guns on IS positions whilst simultaneously negotiating some national unity government[296]. Russia, also an ally of Assad, seems to support the Iranian proposal. Moreover, in September 2015 Moscow sent sophisticated weapons and military advisors to support Assad's beleaguered forces[297]. Sunni Arab states, notably Saudi Arabia and Qatar, and also Turkey are vehemently opposed to the Iranian proposal and to Russian military assistance to Assad's regime. Saudi Foreign Minister

Adel al-Jubeir categorically stated that Assad is not part of the solution but part of the problem and have therefore instead called for Assad's immediate departure from power. Moreover the Saudi Foreign Minister has called for the immediate ending of Tehran's support to Damascus and the departure of all Hezbollah forces from Syria[298].Following the departure of Assad, the Saudi counter-proposal envisaged UN-supervised elections. Needless to say this was not acceptable to Tehran.

The International Response: Russia in Syria and the Intensification of Sectarian Conflict

The alliance between Moscow and Damascus goes back to the 1960s when pro-Soviet Arab nationalists took power[299]. Hafez al Assad (the current president's father) became one of the most reliable clients of Moscow. Putin's Russia has continued to protect their Syrian vassal when in 2011 the rebellion to oust Bashar al Assad began. Moscow made use of its veto in the United Nations (UN) to shield the regime from unified international action on the part of the international community.

On 30 September 2015, however, Moscow ranked up its aid to Assad following a request from Damascus for military assistance[300]. 28 combat aircraft, including 4 Sukhoi Su-30 fighters, 12 Su-25 aircraft, 12 Su-24 attacks fighters, and numerous attack helicopters soon found their way to Syria[301]. Moscow's subsequent aerial campaign began in earnest in early October 2015 with various IS command and control centres and munition depots struck according to Moscow. However, there is reason to doubt the Russian claims. According to the US State Department and NATO, more than 90 percent of Russia's airstrikes have not been directed either against IS or al-Qaeda affiliated terrorists but rather Western-supported rebel formations[302].

The fact that Moscow has also deployed its marines from the 810th Independent Naval Infantry Brigade as well as state-of-the-art T-90 tanks, infrastructure development at the Istamo weapons storage complex near al-Sanobar[303] and advanced artillery also suggest that Russia is also planning a ground offensive. Some of the weaponry, however, has raised concerns amongst Western policy-makers since they do not seem appropriate for the fight against Islamic State. Consider here the Russian deployment of surface-to-air missiles. IS has no air assets so why deploy this? The only planes in the air over Syria (besides the Russians and those of the decrepit Syrian air force now) are those of the US-led coalition. In other words, Moscow seems to be more concerned with keeping Assad in power than just the defeat of IS. It should be borne in mind that Assad's tyrannical rule is not only threatened by that of IS but also various other rebel groups. From this perspective, the Russian military's position to target all armed groups not allied to Damascus is problematic in the extreme[304].

At face value, the Russian involvement in the Syrian imbroglio, ostensibly to fight IS makes sense. After all, Russian Muslims make up 16 percent of the population and this will increase to 20 percent of the population by 2020[305]. Moreover, there have been growing signs of radicalization amongst the Moscow's Muslims. Between 1700 and 3000 Russians – largely Muslims from Russia's restive Caucasus - have joined the ranks of various jihadi factions within Syria, including IS and Jabhat al-Nusra[306]. Moreover, one of Islamic State's most senior military commanders is Abu Omar al-Shishani. As was mentioned in Chapter 2 he is of Chechen-Georgian origins[307].

Putin frames this fight against IS as support for Assad – that only Assad's survival will guarantee IS' defeat. Factually, this is problematic. A study by IHS Jane's defence consultancy made clear that of the 982 operations launched by the Syrian regime, only a minuscule 6 percent was targeted at IS. 94 percent was directed at pro-Western rebel forces[308]. In addition, far from being the implacable enemy of IS, Assad also buys oil from Islamic State[309]. In fact, much of the growth of Islamic State in Syria has to do with decisions made by Assad. In 2011, as the democratic uprisings against Asad, gathered momentum, the Syrian regime on 31 May 2011 issued a general amnesty to political prisoners – ostensibly to placate the protest movement. In reality, the amnesty only applied to Islamist extremists whereas the liberal democratic opponents of the regime remained incarcerated. The release of these jihadists were based on a cynical political calculation on the part of Damascus to tar the political opposition against Asad as all being Islamist terrorists and that there were no moderates of a liberal persuasion amongst the opposition. Among those released were Awwad al-Mahklaf who became the local emir of IS in Raqqa and Abu al-Ahir al-Absi who became Islamic State's provincial governor for Homs[310]. It gets worse. One Syrian military intelligence officer, attached to the Military Intelligence Directorate for 12 years who defected, informed journalists that these hardened jihadists were not merely released from prison but Syrian military intelligence armed them, provided them with ammunition and assisted them in forming armed brigades[311]. IS then piggy-backed on these Islamist formations to organize and spread in Syria. This could be one of the worst experiences of blowback in recent times.

Moreover, Assad's minority government of Alawites which represents a mere 12 percent of Syrians whilst 70 percent are Sunni[312] have managed to antagonize these Sunnis through the indiscriminate use of violence including barrel bombs and poisonous chlorine gas attacks and ruthless medieval sieges of towns. Given the sectarian tensions between Sunni and Shi'a, David Blair[313] writes, *"Nothing would be more likely to rally popular support for IS than helping Assad to reconquer Syria. The vision of an army backed by Shi'a Iran and Christian Russia bearing down on Sunnis in the Arabian heartland would fulfil the millenarian fantasies of the most ardent IS zealot. At a stroke its pitiless worldview would seem to be vindicated".*

Assad's continued stay in power, then, is guaranteed to galvanize more support for IS – precisely the opposite goal that Moscow professes to have. More importantly Moscow's intervention will exacerbate the sectarian tensions between Sunni and Shi'a. Russian forces are located in Latakia[314] – in the heartland of the Alawite community and may well come across as defending the ruling Alawites from the majority Sunni population. Russia has also forged closer political, military and intelligence co-operation with Tehran, the Shi'a regime in Baghdad, the Alawite regime in Damascus and the Shi'a and Iranian militant Hezbollah Islamist movement – the so-called 4 + 1 bloc[315]. Sunnis, viewing Russian involvement in Syria, then would logically come to the conclusion that Moscow's intervention is on the side of the Shi'a. In the process, this might serve to drive them further in the arms of IS as explained earlier.

From a military perspective, what the Russians are planning to do defending Assad and increasing his control over Syria seems destined to fail. Assad's forces only control 20 percent of the country[316]. It is unlikely even with the support of Iran and Russia whether he could gain control over the remaining four-fifths of the country. Consider here the following, the Syrian armed forces has dwindled from 250,000 to 125,000 troops and morale is incredibly low[317]. Moreover, during the course of 2015, the Syrian forces, despite the help received from Tehran and pro-Iranian Hezbollah forces have been retreating as various rebel formations have increasingly expanded the territory under their control[318]. Fundamentally, this reflects a deeper political and demographic problem. The minority Alawite regime of Assad constitutes 12 percent of the population. Consequently, the Syrian Armed Forces do not have the manpower to maintain an area they have recaptured from rebel militias[319]. Furthermore, given the weakness of the Russian economy as seen in the downward spiral of the rouble against the dollar, it does raise the pressing question of whether Moscow's Syrian adventure can be sustained given the poor health of the Russian economy.

If Islamic State is not the real targets of Russian aerial bombardments as explained above and if propping Assad's regime up is not sustainable, what then accounts for the Russian involvement in the Syrian quagmire? Some analysts are of the view that this should be seen within the context of a resurgence of Cold War politics between Russia and the West following Moscow's annexation of Ukraine's Crimea in March 2014[320]. Since then the relationship between Moscow and NATO countries have deteriorated to an unprecedented extent with a NATO military build-up in Eastern Europe whilst Russia has been engaging in a massive rearmament programme. Seen through a Cold War lens, then, Russia is supporting the West's enemies in the region – propping up Assad, allying itself with Tehran, whilst using its aerial bombardment to attack pro-Western rebel forces whilst stating that its only objective is to eliminate Islamic State.

There may be three other, more practical reasons, explaining the involvement of Moscow in the Middle East. First, Syrian forces having lost much ground and equipment, Russia's Rosoborone The Rise of the Islamic State export has the ability to sell billions of dollars of military equipment to Syria[321]. A practical demonstration of Russia's firepower would be the best way to promote such sales. Moreover, other countries too like Iran and Iraq, given their proximity to Moscow, could also be convinced to purchase arms from their newfound ally.

Second, Russia has in recent years grown concerned as the Islamic Republic of Iran's influence has spread in Central Asia – a region perceived by Moscow to be of strategic importance to itself. The vast energy reserves of Central Asia only adds to the strategic value of the region. Russian intervention in Syria to support Iran and its allies Assad and Hezbollah would then not only consolidate bilateral ties between Moscow and Tehran, but would, in Moscow's estimation also reduce the potential of Iranian intervention in Russia's sphere of influence – Central Asia[322]. After all, Moscow reasons, Tehran will not wish to antagonize its new-found ally in Syria, not to mention Iran's support for a diplomatic as opposed to military solution to the thorny question of Iran's nuclear ambitions.

Third, Russian active involvement in Syria could also be the result of defending its naval base at the Syrian port of Tartus. The strategic importance of Tartus for Moscow cannot be under-estimated. According to Jonathan Wade[323]'Tartus is *"…the only Mediterranean repair and replenishment spot for its navy, sparing Russian warships the trip back to their Black Sea bases through the Turkish straits. The facility in Tartus could also be an alternative for aerial shipment of goods due to NATO and Ukraine's decision to close its airspace to Russian military aircraft"*.

Given the strategic importance of Tartus for Russian then, Moscow was taken aback when Syrian rebels from the Jaysh al-Fatah (Army of Conquest) which is supported by Qatar, Saudi Arabia and Turkey took control on 25th April 2015 of the town of Jisr al-Shughur. From here the frontline was suddenly moving too close to Tartus[324]. Russian intervention then was motivated to protect its naval facilities at Tartus. This would also explain Moscow's choice of targets. Whilst IS controls most of eastern Syria[325], these were not the targets of Russia's aerial attacks, rather it was those closest to Latakia province where Tartus was located. These Russian targets, then included Idlib, Hama, Latakia and Homs – all adjacent to the regime enclave of Latakia[326].

Foreign involvement in the conflict then has only served to add further complexity to the conflict. Moreover the dressing up of national self interest in anti-Islamic State rhetoric has added further confusion towards developing a coherent international response towards Islamic State. Russian involvement in the conflict together with that of Iran, Shi'a militias and Hezbollah has also given added impetus to IS and has served to confirm its narrative of the conflict and that it alone is standing up for Sunni interests.

So what should be done? How do we end Islamic State's reign of terror?

4 FIGHTING ISLAMIC STATE: A CALL TO ACTION

Abstract:

There is a desperate need to for more comprehensive measures to be adopted in the struggle against the terrorist menace posed by Islamic State. These include such political measures as exploiting Islamic State's tensions with other Islamist groupings like Afghanistan's Taliban and Syria's Jabhat al-Nusra. These political measures would need to be complemented by economic development in countries like Tunisia where poverty is one of the drivers for radicalization amongst the youth. Given the resonance of Islamic State's views amongst Muslims, more effort needs to be placed on a 'doctrinal overhaul' of Islam. This is essential if extremism is to be overcome. A more credible military strategy also needs to be adopted.

Keywords: Taliban, Jabhat al Nusra, extremism, Libya, Tunisia, funding of terrorism

Introduction

Acknowledging the failures, regarding the existing approach does not mean embracing despondency. Rather it is the start of a more pro-active approach towards dismantling the threat posed by Islamic State. Such a pro-active approach would need to embrace traditional counter-terrorism (reactive) measures but at the same time, it would need to go beyond statist (proactive) responses. Incredibly, much counter-terrorism discourses still privileges national security. Within the context of globalization where insecurity anywhere threatens security everywhere this is incredible. Within the context of a credible global terrorist menace that is Islamic State, this is absurd! Perhaps, the easiest first step towards defeating Islamic State is to exploit its own vulnerabilities.

Political Measures: Exploiting Islamic State's Vulnerabilities

IS suffers from various weaknesses and not enough is done to exploit these further. Consider the following IS' oil revenues have fallen to US $2 million per week as a result of US-led airstrikes which have damaged IS' oil infrastructure, especially refineries. In order to pay salaries (estimated to be US $10 million per month) as well as its "state" institutions such as courts, police, media and market regulation, it has increased taxes on employees from 20% to 50%[327]. This coupled with the low salaries the group offers and the fact that IS does not make investments in infrastructure[328] (on account of it being easily targeted and that given the fluid military situation that territory can change hands overnight) has resulted in the decreasing living standards of IS "citizens". In addition food insecurity has risen. Five years ago, 12 million acres of land was farmed. That figure has halved as a direct result of IS. Farmers have been turned into refugees and internally displaced. A similar dynamic is at work in Syria where half of the population of 22 million have been displaced and no longer contributes to the economy. Even more to the point, cultivation of arable land under IS-control has decreased[329]. As Felix Imonti[330] presciently noted, *"If the caliphate cannot provide food and essential services to the people under its control, it faces an insurrection"*. More needs to be done on the part of the international community to channel "citizens'" anger against the IS leadership and ensure that the gulf between IS and the inhabitants of the areas they control is further widened.

IS can also be quite vindictive. Local tribesmen have been jealous of their autonomy and IS had to fight for almost a year to subdue the residents of Deir al-Zour. More than a thousand people, including many IS fighters were killed over this period. As a result, IS has governed the residents here with a heavy hand imposing punitive taxes on harvest, phone lines, water and electricity. As a result residents here have embarked on a guerrilla campaign regularly ambushing IS fighters. Islamic State responded with public executions of residents Deir al-Zour[331]. More needs to be done by the international community to train and arm such local groups to fight IS.

IS also suffers from other weaknesses. Its declaration that its 'caliphate' enjoys primacy over all other Islamist formations has certainly escalated tensions. In Afghanistan, IS aligned groups have beheaded members of the Taliban who refused to take the oath of allegiance to al-Baghdadi setting the basis for a bloody conflict between the Taliban and IS aligned groups in eastern Afghanistan[332]. Incensed by the defection of senior Taliban commanders such as Mullah Abdul Khadim and Hafiz Waheedto IS, the

Taliban's leader, Mullah Akhtar Mohammed Mansoor, wrote an open letter to the IS leader Abu Bakr al-Baghdadi stating, *"The Islamic Emirate [Taliban] does not consider the multiplicity of jihadi ranks beneficial either for jihad or for Muslims. Your decisions taken from a distance will result in the Islamic State losing support of religious scholars, mujahideen ..and in order to defend its achievements the Islamic Emirate will be forced to react"*[333]. In August 2015 tensions between the two organizations once more came to light when IS released a video filmed in eastern Afghanistan depicting eight bound and blindfolded prisoners whom they then blew up with explosives. Interestingly, IS declared all prisoners to be "apostates" aligned to either the Taliban or the Afghan government[334]. It seems that IS drew no distinction between the Taliban and the Afghan government. The Afghan Taliban condemned the "horrific" video and threatened dire consequences for IS[335]. Such rivalries should be exploited by those seeking to end the reign of terror by Islamic State. There is also the economic competition between IS and the Taliban around control over the lucrative drug trade. Afghanistan produces 90 percent of global opium production and is the largest grower of cannabis in the world. The tensions between the Taliban and IS also revolved around controls over this multi-billion dollar drug trade[336].

Similarly, in Syria Jabhat al-Nusra refuses to play second fiddle to IS and has aligned itself with other rebel groupings to take on the forces of al-Baghdadi. As Barnard and Arango[337] asserted about Jabhat al-Nusra, *"They can match the Islamic State in espousing Sunni sectarian views, condemning minority sects, and reject its claim to represent Sunnis, calling themselves instead "khawarej," a term from Islamic history signifying divisive outsiders".* In Syria, IS also ran into trouble with theAhrar al-Sham grouping in Aleppo in 2013. The encroachment of IS on Ahrar al-Sham territory as well as the killing of one of its senior commanders – Abu Rayyan – resulted in Jabhat al-Nusra and Arhar al-Sham joining forces to take on IS. Fighting was intense and IS withdrew from Idlib, Latakia, Hama and Deiraz-Zor provinces[338]. More could be done by the international community to exploit these differences further amongst the Islamists.

Political Measures: Highlighting Islamic State's Atrocities

At one level, as was explained in an earlier chapter, Islamic State is quick to trumpets its military victories as well as the exercise of its soft power, for instance building wells for local communities on social media, in a bid to encourage new recruits to join the Islamists' ranks. At the same time, not enough is being done by the international community to fight Islamic State at this level. This is a grave strategic error.

Consider the following. Between 2014 and 2015, IS has succeeded in recruiting young women to join IS from all over the world. At the same time, IS has a terrible human rights record when it comes to girls and women in the areas they control. Human Rights Watch has meticulously documented systematic and organized rape, sexual assault, sexual slavery and forced "marriages" on girls as young as 12[339]. Indeed sex slavery seems to be quite an IS enterprise with auctions being held where, for instance, captured Yazidi girls are sold for US $2500[340]. Policy-makers need to get more of this information out into the public domain to serve as deterrence to would-be females seeking to join the militant group. This, in practice means, ensuring the hideous stories of those women who have escaped Islamic State's captivity needs to get out more aggressively into mainstream and social media. Resources have to be set aside for this intervention. More specifically, these need to be channeled to those young women most at risk in terms of age group, socio-economic class and geographical area.

Political Measures: An Overarching Strategy which allows for Regional Variations: Lessons from Libya

It is also important to understand that whilst there is a need for an overarching strategy to respond to IS, it should allow for regional variations. Just as IS adapts their techniques to local contexts, so too must counter-terrorism strategies adapt to regional and local contexts. Thus, whilst Iraq and Syria would need to be broken up for reasons outlined earlier, Libya, on the other hand is a country in desperate need for a functioning central authority. To this end the international community needs to focus their attention on getting the two rival "governments" in Tripoli and Tobruk to forge a government of national unity. In October 2014, UN Secretary-General Ban Ki-moon did attempt to broker talks between the rivals but this failed to end the impasse[341]. Other efforts by the world body under the able leadership of the UN Special Envoy for Libya, Bernadino Leon, continued throughout 2015. On 20th September 2015 the deadline for establishing a unity government came and went[342] with no end insight of the impasse. Renewed efforts are now needed but greater pressure in the form of both carrot and stick on the part of the international community must now come into play to force Tripoli and Tobruk to cooperate in the face of a common existential threat posed by IS.

There are some who believe that like in the case of Iraq and Syria, one should also accept the divisions between the Tripoli and Tobruk and accept that there may be two or even three Libyan states emerging. One proponent of this view is Gal Luft who passionately argued that, "*Sometimes a divided country is better than a broken and hopeless one*"[343]. There are several problems however with this position. First, unlike in Iraq and Syria there are no Sunni, Shia or Kurdish groups populating a particular area and in *de facto* in control over it. Second, Libya has a multiplicity of clans whose concept of the national interest does not go beyond their village's boundaries. The various clan militias operating throughout the country each have their own little fiefdom. At last count (in August 2015) there were a staggering 1,700 militias in this strife-torn country[344]. In such a situation there is no possibility of developing a coherent policy against IS which operates throughout the length and breadth of Libya. Third, to make matters worse, some of these militias are allied to Tripoli others to Tobruk. The two rival administrations in Libya then serve to reinforce the clan divisions and vice versa. Thus, once the primary fault-line between the two rival administrations in Tripoli and Tobruk is overcome, it is imperative that these rival militias are coerced or cajoled to disband and become part of a new national armed force. This, of course, cannot occur without the support of the international community. Accepting a divided Libya, then, is tantamount to giving IS' Libyan franchise a blank check – to operate with impunity.

Second, the international arms-embargo which was imposed in 2011[345] must end and weapons must get to the proposed government of national unity urgently. We have already seen that elements of Libya's armed forces can fight if properly resourced. In December 2014, for instance they captured most of Benghazi and the approaches to Derna from IS[346]. Seven months later – in July 2015 – IS was expelled from Derna despite them sending additional fighters as reinforcements from Tunisia, Yemen and other Arab states[347]. The lessons from Derna is quite important if Islamic State is to be defeated. IS has made use of the sectarian Sunni-Shiite divide very successfully in Iraq and Syria. In Libya, a wholly Sunni country it had considerably less room to maneuver given the absence of such sectarian tensions IS has done so well to exploit. Islamic State's decision to send in more foreign jihadis, meanwhile, served only to exacerbate the alienation from local residents. Libya is notoriously a closed society, even xenophobic. This resulted in the citizens of Derna taking to the streets protesting against the presence of foreigners. When IS opened fire on these protestors, killing seven, the local Al Qaeda-aligned militia – the Abu Salim Martyrs Brigade – made common cause with government forces in retaking Derna from IS control[348]. In August 2015, IS began a fresh offensive on Derna with a series of suicide car bombings. These, however, were indiscriminate in nature and resulted in large civilian casualties[349] – turning the residents even more firmly against IS. Derna was clearly a strategic blunder for IS. Derna, was indicative of how IS could be ousted – when local militias together with government forces united and are supported by the general populace.

However, being forced out of Derna, IS has entrenched itself in Sirte – Gaddafis' hometown where many disaffected Gaddafi loyalists have congregated[350]. This compelled what is left of the Libyan Air Force to engage in aerial strikes against IS targets from their Tripoli base[351], attempting to take out much of IS command and control facilities in Sirte. However, given the fact that IS has consolidated its control over Sirte, it would suggest that the aerial campaign was an abject failure. Since June 2015, IS has taken control over the city's power plant, television and radio stations, the hospital and the university. Sirte's former Internal Security building, meanwhile has become the militant group's command centre[352]. Other Islamist militias in Sirte, such as Ansar al-Sharia and MajlisShuraShabab al-Islam, have been compelled to pledge allegiance to IS leader Abu Bakr al-Baghdadi[353].

If the lessons, from Derna were quite positive in the sense of how to defeat the Islamists, the lessons from Sirte is equally stark on what not to do. As in post-Saddam Hussein Iraq, where with the encouragement of Washington, Baathist generals were dismissed and Sunnis were largely marginalized in the Shia-dominated Baghdad, a similar development had occurred in Libya. Members of Gaddafi's clan as well as senior military officers were not incorporated into governing structures of Libya. These soon made common cause with Islamic State. The capture of Sirte, then, was a spectacular failure on the part of post-Gaddafi Libyan political elites to not govern in an inclusive manner. From a policy perspective, then, the proposed government of national unity must revoke the 2013 law which forbids former Gaddafi officials from holding public office[354] in a bid to woo former officers of the Gaddafi regime away from IS and towards the new inclusive government.

Whilst Libyans focus on Derna and Sirte and the Europeans grow apprehensive with the black flag of the militants being raised on Europe's doorstep, the jihadis have again demonstrated an ability to play the ball wide – keeping their enemies guessing as to their next move. IS has now focused on the impoverished south where neither rival Libyan government has any authority in the area. Here they have taken advantage of the lethal clashes between rival tribes – Tuaregs and Tebu and have sided with Tuaregs and have succeeded in recruiting them as fighters[355]. Once again, this underlines the need for a single government authority in Libya which can effectively exercise its authority across the length and breadth of its territory. Once more it highlights the need for inclusive governance. Because Tuaregs played a prominent role in the Gaddafi military machine, political elites in the new Libya were sympathetic with the Tebu. This, then, resulted in

Islamic State exploiting the situation for them to develop a presence in southern Libya. Inclusive governance, then, can be a potent anti-dote to IS which, as has been demonstrated, is quite adept at exploiting sectarian fractures in society.

As has been asserted repeatedly, the current Libyan rival authorities do not have the capacity to take the fight to Islamic State and would need regional and international assistance. The proposed Libyan government of national unity needs to work with other regional players to take the fight to IS. In February 2015, for instance, Egyptian jets bombed IS targets in Derna, following the beheading of 21 Coptic Christians by IS[356]. Such air strikes on the part of the Egyptians, in future, could be coordinated with a ground offensive of a newly revitalized Libyan army. Indeed, the Tobruk-based Libyan government has appealed for international assistance to take the fight to IS[357].

At the international level, the North Atlantic Treaty Organization (NATO) which played such a decisive role in the ouster of Gaddafi[358] has a moral duty and a vested interest to support the Libyans and regional players to put an end to the brutality of IS. What is morally reprehensible and strategically flawed is that the only response to the fall of Sirte emanating from NATO capitals is a joint statement from the United States, France, Germany, Italy, Spain and Britain stating, *"We are deeply concerned about reports that these [IS] fighters have shelled densely populated parts of the city [Sirte] and committed indiscriminate acts of violence to terrorize the Libyan population"*[359]. Statements of condemnations and words are not going to defeat IS however. As is the case of the Obama Administration choosing not to put boots on the ground in Iraq, so is it with NATO in Libya. It is time for action on the part of NATO given Libya's strategic location. Sirte, in particular has become a regional headquarters of IS in North Africa, whilst being a stone throw-away from Europe.

Political Measures: Good Governance should also form part of a Comprehensive Counter-Terrorism Strategy: Lessons from Tunisia

If inclusive governance forms part of an antidote to countering Islamic State, so is good governance as the case of Tunisia will demonstrate. Tunisia has suffered the repeated targeting of foreign tourists at museums, archaeological sites and beach resorts. Whilst the deployment of armed tourist security officers along coastal resorts, in hotels and museums might be most useful in the short-term, ultimately, prevention is better than cure. Part of a sustainable prevention strategy is the cultivation of human intelligence assets to disrupt terrorist attacks whilst still in the planning phase. However much more is needed for a comprehensive counter-terrorism prevention strategy.

Current Tunisia counter-terrorism policy is problematic to say the least. Part of the problem is structural in nature and goes back to the period immediately following independence when Tunisia's first president – Habib Bourguiba – fearful of military coups, deliberately starved the army of resources. This policy continued under his successor Zine el-Abidine Ben Ali who whilst starving the military of funds, developed a strong police force which was loyal to him personally[360]. Fast forward to 2011 when Ben Ali was ousted by a popular uprising and the new administration inherited a small and ill equipped army and a police force which was largely disbanded and had to be reconstituted on a professional basis[361]. Given Tunisia's proximity to Europe, the North Atlantic Treaty Organization (NATO) could assist Tunisia's armed forces with equipment and training whilst individual countries such as France, the former colonial power, could play a significant role in assisting Tunisia's moribund police force.

Tunisia's current counter-terrorism policy also lacks coherence and imagination. Following the attack on the beach resort at Sousse in June 2015, Prime Minister Habib Essid announced the erection of a new border wall[362] - in the process ignoring the fact that the perpetrators of the Sousse attack were home-grown radicals and not foreigners. Similarly, the announcement of by Essid that 80 radical mosques will be closed is equally problematic given the fact that the perpetrator of the Sousse attack was radicalized online[363]. The closure of such mosques will only serve to drive radical Islam underground making it more difficult to detect whilst at the same time reinforcing the IS narrative that Islam itself is under attack. An effective counter-terrorism strategy, then is one which also seeks to fast-track Tunisian youth into employment. The closure of 80 mosques, meanwhile, also plays into the strategy of IS as previously outlined where they seek to force the government to over-react thereby alienating more of its citizens – those who are pious Muslims - but who are not necessarily Islamist in orientation. It is a particularly poor strategy in view of the fact that the moderate Islamists of Ennahda are part of the coalition government. Such a strategy therefore, risks causing political instability and undermine the hard-won working relationship forged between moderate Islamists and secularists in the aftermath of the Arab Spring. Neither does the current counter-terrorism strategy seek to explore the structural reasons for the more than 3,000 Tunisian youth who have joined IS and who are acutely susceptible to IS propaganda. Whilst unemployment in Tunisia is standing at a staggering 31 percent. Youth unemployment is much higher than the national average[364].

The Tunisian study also highlights another important facet of a comprehensive counter-terrorism strategy – starting with the acknowledgement of the underlying structural conditions driving recruitment into IS. Across the Middle East and Africa, are large number of disaffected young men who suffer harsh authoritarian rule and little prospect of finding employment[365]. As a result, they cannot get married or start a family. This is of huge cultural significance especially in the Middle East. IS, through its social media campaign highlights the failures of government to provide employment to these young men emphatically arguing that these young men have not failed – rather governments have failed them. Such a message is warmly received by these disaffected young men. Furthermore, IS not only provides paid employment but also provides young men with brides and pays for their honeymoons. Defeating IS, Daniel Cohen and Danielle Levin[366] rightly concludes entails far more than defeating the group militarily. It also encompasses putting pressure on oppressive governments in the region to open up the political process and to overhaul economies to open up economic opportunities for the youth in particular.

Political Measures: Countering Extremism: The Ideological Struggle

In a penetrating analysis, Joseph Nye[367] argues that Islamic State is actually three things – a transnational terrorist group, a proto-state, and a political ideology with religious roots. The former two can be defeated by means of robust and sustained counter-terrorism measures. But, if the ideological roots of Salafi jihadism is not removed, a new IS will emerge a decade or two later. Indeed, this has been the pattern as was explained in Chapter 3. As has been repeatedly stressed, the ideology of IS finds resonance amongst almost a fifth of Muslims worldwide. The importance of counter-radicalization strategy, in this context, cannot be stressed enough. It is however, important to recognize that such a strategy needs to be cast wider than the violent extremism of IS. There is after all a distinct linkage between non-violent extremism and violent extremism with groups like Jamaat al-Tablighwal- Da'wa (Society for Propagation and Preaching), which has a `quietist' and non-political image, playing a crucial role in the radicalization and recruitment of Muslims for the Islamist cause[368]. As a result, authorities' should focus their attention on stopping non-violent extremism from morphing into violent extremism.

The importance of ideological indoctrination for IS' overall strategy cannot be overstated. Between September 2014 and August 2015, 15,000 IS fighters were estimated to be killed by the American-led coalition airstrikes.

At the same time however, via online recruitment, IS managed to replenish their ranks by a further 30,000 recruits. Radicalization and recruitment therefore managed to more than offset the deaths of their fighters and, consequently, the organization actually grew over this period[369]. The battle for ideas and imagery, then, as *The Economist*[370] asserted is as vital as the military battles taking place in Iraq and Syria. Under the circumstances various Western governments have urged internet firms to close IS-linked accounts. These, of course, will spring up again. For this reason, governments worldwide should focus on resourcing those agencies tasked to keep bringing down IS-linked accounts. In addition more capacity is needed within governments to take down botnets[371]. Botnets is where a number of internet computers without their owners' knowledge have been set up to forward transmissions to other computers generally through a Trojan virus[372].In this way, IS spreads its propaganda and is extremely difficult to remove. The US government has also engaged in counter-IS propaganda putting out videos on You Tube, for instance, highlighting the atrocities committed by the terrorist organization[373]. In terms of sheer volume, these however, hardly match the jihadis own prolific outputs. Thus, more resources needs to be allocated to beat Islamic State at its own game.

In addition, both the US and Britain agreed to go after members of Islamic State's Cyber Caliphate, such as British citizen and hacker, Junaid Hussain who played a crucial role in inciting Western Muslims to engagein lone-wolf terror attacks. In August 2015, Hussain was killed in Syria in a US-airstrike[374]. Rafaello Pantucci of the London-based Royal United Services Institute is of the opinion that such targeting will not seriously damage IS in the medium to long-term, *"Undoubtedly his [Junaid Hussain] online skills we be missed by the group; but it is unlikely to dramatically change the pattern of dangerous plots emanating from the group, or the phenomenon of some young Westerners being drawn to fight alongside the group"*[375].

In other social media platforms Western and Arab governments have encouraged the spread of a more moderate Islam by getting religious leaders to denounce IS as distorting the teachings of Islam[376]. In Egypt, for instance, the House of Fatwa, the country's leading Islamic authority and organ of state has launched various social campaigns demonstrating how IS has, in their view, distorted the teachings of Islam[377]. There are however several problems with such a strategy. First, as was explained the IS narrative is intimately grounded in Islamic traditions. Second, a large number of Muslims around the world find the ideology of the group appealing. Third, it seems counter-intuitive to make use of Muslim religious leaders to speak to a group who believe that these very religious leaders have strayed from the true Islamic path. To put it differently, IS members believe they possess the true Islam. Fourth, there is a real danger that if Western and Arab governments pursue this strategy, moderate Islam itself may become discredited as it is perceived to have been co-opted by Westerners or corrupt and authoritarian Arab rulers.

This, however, is not an argument not to make use of these religious leaders to counter the IS narrative, rather it is an appeal that such Muslim scholars and preachers used must not be perceived to also lose their independence, they must also be critical of Western governments - for example their role in the Middle East imbroglio. A moderate Islam, then, must not be uncritical of the actions of the West as well as the despotism of Arab elites. A moderate Islam which lambasts the atrocities of IS and is silent on the follies of Western government or draconian Arab rule would have scant appeal to the mass of Muslims globally. So what would a moderate Islam look like? Given the fact that IS quotes from the Qur'an and certain Prophetic traditions, EbrahimMoosa[378] calls for a `doctrinal overhaul' of Islam – one which negates the Salafist rejection of interpretation of scriptural sources. Building on authentic Islamic traditions, Azizur Rahman Patel has cogently called for the `de-Islamisation of politics'[379], which not only seeks to neutralize the cultural tendency to enforce Islamic codes of morality and religious adherence in the public domain' but also to support `those societal groupings that appropriate and employ more contextual readings of Islamic principles of justice, liberty, and equality, and compatibility with other cultures and civilizations of the world'[380].The need to move away from a dogmatic, literal Islam which lends itself to justify decapitations, sexual slavery and war towards one which is regarded as an organic text, a living Qur'an if you wish adapting to the needs of particular peoples is also one called for by Cawo Abdi. In keeping for a need for a critical Islam though Abdi cogently argues that, *"It will require a revolutionary Muslim introspection to reclaim Islam for future generations. Such introspection would not only reject and mobilize again extremists' fossilized and doomed version of Islam but also against Western-backed brutal dictatorial regimes in the Islamic world that use the war on terror to terrorize their own citizens as well as Western neo-imperial policies and projects"*[381].

Echoing Cawo Abdi, Abdel Bari Atwan[382] has succinctly noted, *"IS, like al-Qaeda, is perceived by many Muslims as fighting the `crusaders' who seek to invade and exploit the resources of Muslim lands. And while the west decries IS violence, its rough justice and its subjugation of women, many in the Muslim world are profoundly conscious of the hypocrisy involved here: the deaths of hundreds of thousands of Iraqi, Afghan, Yemeni and Pakistani citizens in US bombardments and drone strikes; the torture and abuse of Muslim prisoners in detention facilities like Abu Ghraib where water boarding and `rectal rehydration' (anal rape with a water hose) were commonplace…"* What is needed is a critical and assertive Islam providing a critique against the atrocities of IS and the violation of human rights perpetrated by the West in Muslim countries too. To do the former and not the latter would delegitimize any attempt to reform Islam from within.

Revising Islamic doctrine is one thing but there is still the problem of the sense of purpose young people get from embarking on jihad – Islamic State-style. Bobby Ghosh suggested this desire to be a part of something larger amongst young Muslims can be met if a Muslim Peace Corps could be established. US President John F. Kennedy created the Peace Corps in the 1960 and more than 200,000 young American men and women volunteers have served amongst the poor and distressed in 140 countries. Ghosh suggests that this could fall under the Organization of the Islamic Conference (OIC) which was established in 1969 and whose aim is to build solidarity amongst Muslim nations[383]. Under such a programme an Egyptian youth could undergo a 3 month period of vocational training and then sent off to do humanitarian work in Indonesia for two years. This could serve two purposes. First provide that sense of purpose. Second, it could assist with unemployed Muslim youth to acquire the necessary skill-sets and experience to make them more employable when the return to their respective countries.

To counter the radical narratives emanating from IS one needs to acknowledge that there are structural conditions, as was explained with Tunisia, which provide the fertile ground where these extremist ideologies take root. In Europe, surveys demonstrate that 39 percent of Muslims Europeans are poor and at least 13 percent are alienated from their broader society[384]. This make these susceptible to the vicious vitriol emanating from IS. A holistic counter-radicalization strategy, then, seeks not only to challenge the radical narratives itself but also seeks to alleviate the structural conditions which serve to reinforce such narratives.

When discussing these structural conditions an important caveat needs mentioning. Those at risk of IS radicalization are not only Muslims. In England, for instance, English natives who are Christian and even atheists are finding the narrative of IS attractive[385]. This was underlined by the fact that before leaving Britain to join IS, two 22-year-olds from Birmingham purchased a copy of *"The Koran for Dummies"*[386]. In similar fashion, Sally Jones, a 45 year-old former punk rock musician from south-eastern England, who expressed no prior interest in any religion, has also joined IS in Syria in 2015[387]. How does one account for this phenomenon? Writing in The Guardian, Pankaj Mishra[388] cogently argues that, *"Islamic State is often called 'medieval' but is in fact very modern – a horrific expression of a widespread frustration with a globalized western model that promises freedom and prosperity to all, but fails to deliver… The early post-Cold War consensus – that bourgeois democracy has solved the riddle of history, and a global capitalist economy will usher in worldwide prosperity and peace – lies in tatters".*

This popular disaffection, especially amongst the youth, is seen in the large numbers of people choosing not to vote and the anti-austerity protests across Europe. Alienation is also evinced in Occupy Wall Street and Black Lives Matter movements. During the Cold War, which was also a battle of ideologies, the West could rightly compare their economic wealth with the poverty created by "scientific socialism". The West could rightly compare their freedoms with the authoritarianism wrought by Communism. In 2015 the West's political and economic liberalism has scant appeal amongst the disenchanted 99 percent to paraphrase the Occupy Wall Street movement. This will make Islamic State's social media outreach all the harder to counter. IS gives these alienated youth a cause, an identity thereby meeting certain psychological needs whilst at the same time paying them a salary to meet their material needs.

It should also be noted that there is a strong inter-play between terrorist narratives and the state of play on the battlefield. Islamic State is serving to win hearts and mind on account of their military victories on the ground – now controlling an area the size of Britain. As *The Economist* opined, *"Nothing would be so devastating to their propaganda as a sound military defeat"*[389]. The need for a sound military defeat to debunk their ideological narratives is also important from a Muslim theological perspective. One of the three ways in which a caliphate can be established and legitimated is by right of military conquest[390]. Conversely, then, a sound military defeat would undermine that legitimacy.

Political Measures: Going beyond the State

There is yet another aspect of a truly global counter-terrorism strategy we need to revisit and this relates to the efficacy of our global security architecture. Whilst IS has sleeper cells in dozens of countries and its "battalions" consist of several nationalities, the same cannot be said of the international response to what is a looming global threat. Indeed the so-called international response is actually state-based. Organizations like the United Nations, the North Atlantic Treaty Organization or the African Union are all state-based. There is a pressing need to create a truly global security structure. At the moment, IS' global operations is giving them a distinct strategic advantage. Note how IS embattled fighters in Libya called for assistance and received this from Raqqa as well as from local IS-affiliated franchises in Algeria and Tunisia. One US intelligence official alluded to this by noting, *"While the world is watching videos of beheadings and crucifixions in Iraq and Syria the Islamic State is moving into North Africa and the Middle East, and now we see it has a strategy in south Asia. It's a magician's trick; watch this hand and you'll never see what the other is doing"*.[391] At the moment, IS has the strategic advantage not those seeking to defeat this terrorist menace. We live in a globalizing world, where security everywhere is threatened by insecurity anywhere. We cannot fight twenty-first century terrorism with nineteen century structures. The state has to give way to a truly global security architecture.

What would a truly global security architecture combating terrorism look like? First, build on existing truly global legislation. For instance, there is UN Security Council Resolution 2170 which calls on all Member States to prevent the movement of foreign fighters to IS as well as to take measures to staunch the flow of financial and other support to Islamists in Iraq and Syria[392]. Such legislation must be enforced amongst all Member States. Where states, for instance, those in Sub-Saharan Africa do not have the capacity to enforce it, the international community would need to step in to assist them from training to providing them with the necessary hardware to, for instance, maintain a database of those entering and leaving ports of entry. Penalties should, however, be placed on those Member States, who through willful neglect or the lack of the requisite political will refuse to enforce such international legislation.

Second, build on existing regional arrangements. Consider here the European Union (EU). Whilst some Member States of the EU have the firepower to take on IS, others do not. Not all those who do possess the requisite firepower plan to use it to take on IS, while others who intend to take on Islamic State only wish to deploy such firepower in Iraq but not Syria. There are also different national strategic cultures amongst EU Member States in relation to the use of force[393]. There are also growing political differences inside the EU as it relates to Assad. Whilst Britain's David Cameron is closer to the Obama Administration in believing that Assad is part of the problem and has to leave office, Germany's Angela Merkel seems to be vacillating between this position and that of Vladimir Putin – that Assad is needed if Islamic State is to be defeated. Despite the existence, then of an EU Common Security and Defence Policy, there is little "common" amongst EU states when it comes to dealing with IS. In the interest of global security, greater emphasis needs to be place on "common" and less on national strategic interests. The recent waves of migrants engulfing the EU from the Middle East should give Europeans greater reason to develop a unified position on IS which also accords with

UN legislation as seen in UN Security Council Resolution 2170.

Third, the state with its finite resources is overstretched when confronted with the global and multi-faceted nature of an Islamic State. Increasingly, then counter-terrorism has to involve non-state actors as well. Consider here the activities of GhostSec, a division of the hacker group Anonymous. In April 2015 they began attacking hundreds of Islamic State website and thousands of social network accounts used by IS in an effort to stop the jihadis from spreading their propaganda and thereby attract recruits. Within a matter of weeks, GhostSec attacked 233 IS websites, destroyed 85 of these websites and terminated 25,000 Twitter accounts linked to the terrorist group[394]. The company Twitter is also actively involved here. Since the company's policy forbids, "...*direct, specific threats of violence against others,*" and since IS-linked Twitter account violates this policy, Twitter has been suspending 2000 IS-linked accounts per week[395]. The activities of GhostSec and Twitter is an important force-multiplier in the fight against IS indoctrination through social media.

At the same time some intelligence agencies have criticized the activities of GhostSec and Twitter arguing that the eradication of these websites and twitter accounts also prevents them from gathering valuable information concerning IS activities[396]. This criticism, however, should not detract from the amazing work GhostSec and Twitter is doing. This work goes beyond merely taking down websites and social media accounts. In July 2015, Michael Smith an advisor to the US Congress revealed that two terrorist attacks – one in New York and the other in Tunis – was foiled by authorities following the information being gleaned of IS websites by GhostSec who then passed on this information to the authorities in the respective countries[397]. This led to the arrest of 17 terror suspects[398]. Far from being threatened by the sterling work of GhostSec and Twitter, government intelligence agencies should create an interface for greater coordination with these non-state actors so that their activities complement each other in a unified fight against Islamic State.

Fourth, we need to accept that even in the sacred realm of realists – that of combat – the state does not have the monopoly of coercive force over its territory that it once did. This is especially true on the African continent. Consider here the case of Nigeria's Boko Haram now part of Islamic State's West Africa Wilayat. 40,000 Nigerian troops were deployed against Boko Haram to no avail. Nigeria's Islamists captured schoolchildren as in Chibok as sex slaves. They murdered innocent villagers with impunity and Nigeria's armed forces were powerless to halt this carnage. Recognizing the disorganized and demoralized nature of his own army, Nigerian President

Goodluck Jonathan hired a private military company – Specialized Tasks, Training, Equipment and Protection (STTEP) run by former South African Colonel Eben Barlow in January 2015[399]. Barlow, in turn, brought in an elite strike task group consisting of 100 veterans of South Africa's border wars 30 years ago as well as helicopter pilots flying their own combat missions.

Remarkably these counter-insurgency specialists were in their 50s and 60s. Despite their age, they managed to push Boko Haram back out of several towns in a relatively short period of time whilst at the same time allowing for relatively peaceful conditions in northern Nigeria in which to hold an election. How was this accomplished? Recognizing that the Nigerian armed forces were largely using conventional warfare tactics against Boko Haram specializing in asymmetric warfare, STTEP imitated Boko Haram's own guerrilla-style tactics with non-stop assaults labelled "relentless pursuit". Using their own trackers from South Africa's bush wars in Namibia, STTEP could tell in which direction the militants were heading, how fast they were going and from the loads they were carrying the kind of weapons they had in their possession. Helicopters would then carry the STTEP strike force ahead of Islamists. At the same time gun crews on the helicopters were given "kill blocks" to the front and flanks of the strike force. Boko Haram was defeated in every one of these engagements with STTEP[400]. The only member of the strike force to have been killed was 59-year-old Leon Lotz who was killed by friendly fire – from a Nigerian tank[401]. In addition to these direct combat operations, STTEP advised Nigerian security forces, they assisted with gathering intelligence on Boko Haram, flew Nigerian troops into theatres of operation and also assisted with the evacuation of casualties[402].

Despite their great success against Nigeria's Islam State-aligned terrorists, members of STTEP face criminal prosecution in South Africa. South Africa's Minister of Defence Nosiviwe Mapisa-Nqakula labelled these men "mercenaries" and declared that their deployment to Nigeria is illegal under the countries legislation[403]. Given the malevolent role mercenaries played in post-independence Africa, one can understand her wariness. However, these are changed circumstances. Islamist terrorists were and are wreaking havoc in Nigeria. Government forces failed to halt the carnage. Regional forces in the form of the Economic Community of West African States (ECOWAS) also failed. The much-vaunted African Standby Force (ASF) of the African Union (AU), meanwhile, remains a paper-tiger[404]. Under these circumstances, the legitimate government of Nigeria called on an African private military company for assistance.

Given the enormity of the terrorist threat confronted on the African continent, given the weakness of African states militarily to confront this threat, surely it would make sense for African governments to partner with private military companies in the way the Nigerian government did? Whilst human rights groups may well ask whether these companies are publicly accountable and the like, the reality is who speaks for the countless victims of terrorism on this continent? In addition one could examine the creation of a regulatory mechanism providing oversight over such private military companies. In addition, one should also note that these companies often have a code of conduct for themselves as well. Colonel Eben Barlow has noted that STTEP's code of conduct compels it to act in "...*a legal, moral and ethical manner*"[405]. The purpose of such a regulatory mechanism will ensure that the code of conduct is enforced and does not contradict international law – for example, the Geneva Conventions regulating war.

Fifth, there is a need for smart partnerships to develop between governments and the business community throughout the world. It was former US Secretary of Defence Donald Rumsfeld who stressed the involvement of the business sector in the global fight against terrorism when he asserted that, *"The uniforms in this conflict will be bankers' pinstripes and programmers' grunge just as assuredly as desert camouflage"*[406]. Government security services suffering resource constraints can develop synergies with the business sector that have a vested interest to also move into the counter-terrorism domain.

Large multi-national corporations because of their international footprint and their wealth have increasingly come to be seen as high-value targets by terrorist groups. Another target for terrorists is the critical infrastructure of a country. In the United States, 85 percent of the country's critical infrastructure is owned by the private sector[407]. In the US, then, public-private counter-terrorism partnerships should logically focus on protection for key infrastructure. In countries such as South Africa, where the police services are over-stretched with criminality and where no equivalent to a Department of Homeland Security exists, the private sector can play a key role as a force multiplier. After all private security guards outnumber the police by a ratio of 4:1. In addition, the tens of thousands of closed circuit cameras operated by the private sector are not only useful against criminals but also terrorists[408].

The business sector can play a major role in cutting off the money flow to terrorist organizations. After all, more than US $1 trillion is crossing borders each and every day. Given the magnitude of these money transfers, state institutions need the assistance of financial institutions to track terrorist financing. Since the 9/11 terror attacks banks, brokerage firms, wire transfer services, mutual funds and even casinos have played a key role in alerting governments of potential cases of terrorist financing and stopping such transfers from taking place[409].

An important contribution to counter-terrorism measures by the business sector is innovation. It is after all pharmaceutical companies which are responding to creating anti-dotes to potential biological and chemical attacks. Reflecting on business innovations in an era of global terrorism, Murray Weidenbaum[410] notes:

"Northrop Grumman believes that some of its advanced technology can be used in developing difficult-to-forge "smart cards" containing biometric and other personal identification information. Raytheon is experimenting with advanced communications equipment that would help direct police, fire, and medical personnel in responding to terrorist attacks. Boeing is studying whether sensors designed to track missiles could be used to identify hijacked airlines; the company obtained a major order (in excess of $500 million) to install and maintain explosive-detecting equipment at US airports. Lockheed Martin has won contracts to train the newly federalized workforce of airport baggage and passenger screeners. It also received a contract to redesign airport security checkpoints to accommodate new metal detectors and federal screeners".

Such public-private sector partnerships could also extend into intelligence sharing. Multinational corporations have over the years perfected the field of risk analysis. Large corporations, consequently track a variety of risk factors which may negatively impact on their profits margins. Such data, however, could also assist governments in the mitigation of terrorism. In addition, companies increasingly keep track of customers and visitors on their premises as well as undertake background checks on newly recruited staff[411]. In order to facilitate this intelligence-sharing, Stacy Neal[412] urges the establishment of formal cross-sector communication channels between the business sector and government departments to assist the timely transfer of information to policy makers. As with private military companies, however, this interaction between corporations and governments are not without their problems. There are fears around information security and privacy concerns as well as increased government regulation over the private sector[413].

These problems are however not insurmountable. At the end of the day both governments and corporations are targeted by a common enemy: international terrorism. It is therefore in their common interest to work together in mitigating and eradicating the threat posed. From this perspective, the establishment of a cross-sector communication channel and establishing the rules by which such a mechanism will operate could serve as a confidence-building mechanism between corporations and government departments active in the security sector. Moreover, *"Bridge-*

building organizations in academia or the non-profit world can facilitate this cooperation by acting as a synthesis point for both private-sector needs and ideas and public-sector policy development"[414].

Economic Measures: Ending the Financing of Terrorism

The financing of IS needs to be curbed. Finances is the terrorist group's oxygen. As was mentioned IS' imposes taxes on locals in the areas they control. Unfortunately, public servants in Iraq and Syria living in IS-controlled areas, continue to receive salaries from the central government[415]. Indirectly then through the taxes imposed on civil servants, the governments in Baghdad and Damascus are financing IS. Here Aymenn Jawad Al-Tamimi[416] proposes that these governments should compensate public servants, *"...in IS-held areas in goods which are less liquid than cash as a way to stifle income without virtually depriving the population of its livelihood".*

Given the role of Saudi and Gulf charities, in particular, in promoting Islamist extremism, Tarek Fatah proposes putting an end to cash donations to mosques from these entities[417]. At the same time it must be acknowledged that there are positive steps being taken by some of these countries as well. Kuwait has established a financial intelligence centre and Qatar has enacted legislation regulating the fundraising of charities[418]. The establishment of this financial centre and enacting of legislation is one issue. In order to assess its effectiveness we will need to see if the legislation is truly enforced and if terror financiers are prosecuted. For much too long the adoption of legislative frameworks have not resulted in prosecutions for those financially supporting terror networks. Given the role of Ankara and Riyadh in supporting IS, further pressure needs to be placed on these capitals to play a more constructive role in eradicating the threat stemming from Islamic State.

Despite the criticism of US-led airstrikes, it must also be acknowledged that it has served to financially hurt IS. Coalition airstrikes have served to provide the aerial cover necessary for Iraqi troops to recapture the Baiji refinery just north of Mosul in October 2014. Further US airstrikes on IS-controlled oil pipelines has also resulted in IS oil-production falling from 70,000 barrels of crude oil to 25,000 barrels per day[419]. Turkey is also now coming under pressure from Washington to close off its routes to Islamic State oil[420].

Given the financial support to IS by sympathizers as per the confiscated millions found at Johannesburg airport, more needs to be done to ensure that monies do not reach Islamic State and that those willing to financially support terrorist entities are prosecuted to the full extent of the law as a means to deter those financing terrorism. Legislation already exists to empower states to act in this manner. UN Security Council Resolution 1373, for instance, calls on member states to deny all forms of financial support for terrorist groups[421]. What is needed however is that this needs to be enforced and heavier penalties needs to be imposed on terrorist financiers. In the case of South Africa despite several instances of citizens financing terrorism, no prosecution for such action has occurred[422]. Where states lack the political will to undertake such measures despite the fact that they are signatories to such counter-terror legislation, they must be made to pay a price by the international community.

Military Measures: Revisiting the 'Boots on the Ground' Debate

In the previous chapter the folly of a strategy of aiming to decapitate the leadership of IS was examined. In itself, such an approach at eliminating the senior leadership would merely deal temporary blows to the terrorist organization. To do serious damage to these jihadis what is needed is sustained targeted assassinations aimed at eliminating entire managerial layers within IS. Given the wilayat or provincial structure of governance alluded to earlier, this would mean the elimination of the administrative emir and his entire administrative committee in a particular region[423].

This strategy, however, presumes that one has knowledge about the group's personnel, organization and activities. Acquiring IS computer hard drives, memory sticks and other records as well as eliminating IS managers, in turn, requires the use of US Special Forces. President Obama, however, has expressed no desire to deploy Special Forces in this manner. Currently the small number of US forces are only providing Iraqi troops with training and acting as advisor to Iraqi ground forces[424] as well as advising moderate Syrian rebel forces. In other words, even if Washington does not want to deploy ground forces in sufficient numbers to take on IS, at the very least, they should allow the deployment of Special Forces to acquire computer devices and the like for the elimination of IS managerial layers. Failure to do this will result in IS continuing to expand. Veteran US Senator John McCain at a Senate hearing in July 2015 forthrightly stated the obvious when he declared that Islamic State was winning at present[425].

The issue of ground forces however still needs to be revisited. Even if IS' conventional forces are ejected from an area through a combination of airstrikes and a ground offensive, they would shift to tactics of infiltration and assassination. For this reason a ground force of sufficient numbers is required to hold the territory liberated. Currently, US-led airstrikes is serving to assist Iranian proxy forces – whether Hezbollah in Syria or Shi'a militias in Iraq[426]. As alluded to in the previous chapter it makes no sense for Sunni extremists to be ejected in favour of Shi'a extremists. At the same time, this is not an argument for American military presence which might well be viewed as a foreign army of occupation as occurred following the ouster of Saddam Hussein. In the previous chapter the case for partitioning Iraq and Syria along Kurdish, Shi'a and Sunni lines was made. A case can be made, then, for a pan-Arab Sunni force made up of those Arab countries of a more moderate disposition such as Jordan to play a key role in providing such ground forces.

Military Measures: Finding More Reliable Allies in the Fight Against Islamic State

Beyond coercing such unreliable allies as Saudi Arabia and Turkey to actually fight the extremists, the US also finds itself in an unlikely *de facto* alliance with Iran – a designated state sponsor of terrorism. As was explained earlier, Iran has made use of the chaos engulfing Iraq and Syria to expand its influence in the Middle East. Iranian-aligned Shi'a militias in Iraq and Iranian-sponsored Hezbollah forces are benefitting from US aerial strikes to expand the territories they respectively control in Iraq and Syria. Far from allying itself with any Islamist extremism in the form of the Iran and its regional surrogates or unreliable "allies" like Saudi Arabia and Turkey, it would be far better for the US to focus its lens on those states in the region, opposed to religious extremism whatever its source. This would include support for Egypt who under President Al-Sisi has demonstrated its resolve to take the fight to the jihadis (after all, the Egyptians are already battling with IS-aligned jihadis in the Sinai), Israel (which has witnessed the emergence of IS in the Gaza Strip as well as having them on the border of the Golan Heights) and Jordan which has demonstrated its resolve to stamp out any form of jihadism developing on its territory.

More assistance needs to be provided to the Kurds to take on Islamic State. The Kurdish cooperation (as opposed to alliance) with Iran, however, remains a pragmatic one and more needs to be done to supply the Kurdish forces with the weapons and training necessary to wean them off their Iranian patrons[427]. Kurdish support, however, as was explained earlier, would not be possible without accepting their right to self-determination. Similarly support from Sunnis would not be attained without accepting their desire to form an independent state. In other words, for the US and the West in general to secure the military support of Kurds and Sunnis, the dismemberment of Iraq and Syria would need to be accepted. At the moment, the political objective of maintaining the fiction of Iraq and Syria's current borders is undermining the military objective of defeating Islamic State.

Then there is the question of support for the moderate Syrian opposition. Some policy-makers and media outlets have been quite sceptical whether these actually exist – that the Syrian political landscape is only dotted by different shades of Islamist extremism. David Patten[428], however, reminds us of the case of Harakat Hazm (Steadfastness Movement) which was formed in January 2014. They had a secular ideology and boasted a credible military wing. Yet, in February 2015, as a result of receiving little Western support, Jabhat al-Nusra overran their headquarters and the movement ceased to exist. David Patten[429] continues, *"If Harakat Hazm no longer exists, that may tell more about the U.S. mismanagement of support than about the group's original potential"*. The lesson then is quite clear: support the secular opposition to Assad more robustly. These are needed not only in the short-term in the fight against IS and Damascus but these moderate forces are needed in a post-Asad, post-Islamic State Middle East if one wishes to arrive at a more sustainable peace.

Then there is the thorny question relating to Russia. As was explained Russia is playing a hugely negative role in the Middle East – propping up Asad, allying itself with Tehran, not targeting IS and striking at pro-Western rebel forces. If Russia and Western nations could come together to strike at Islamic State, the days of the jihadis would be truly numbered. Recognizing the danger of Russian and coalition aircraft flying sorties and to prevent any possibility of and to prevent an incident over Syrian skies occurring between their respective fighter aircraft, both Moscow and Washington has undertaken to conduct military-to-military talks[430]. Russian Foreign Minister Sergey Lavrov has also indicated that he will continue discussions with his US counterpart, Secretary of State John Kerry to enhance cooperation against Islamic State[431]. Russia could play a very positive role given their influence over Damascus. Vladimir Putin could use this influence to nudge Asad to exit the political scene graciously and thereby set the scene for a government of national unity sans Asad[432].However, Putin would need to be incentivised to play a more constructive role. Given the strategic importance of the Russian naval port at Tartus, the international community and Syrian rebels could well guarantee Russia's continued use of Tartus.

5 GAZING INTO THE CRYSTAL BALL

Abstract:

The phenomenon of Islamic State will continue to grow in the short to medium term. Part of the reason for this relates to the fact that the reformation of Islam has largely stalled on account of the fight back from more conservative clerics. Demographic and environmental variables are also serving to fuel religious fundamentalism globally. Given the austerity measures adopted by many Western countries, security forces are not properly resourced to take on the challenge posed by these global jihadis. As a result, European security officials pessimistically believe that it is only a matter of time when terrorism once again strikes their cities. The Islamic State franchise is going global with 17 regional affiliates and 60 sleeper cells around the world.

Keywords: Islamic reformation, under-resourced security forces, Islamic State's organizational structure, demographics

Introduction

Despite the recommendations to end the reign of terror of IS contained in the previous chapter, the reality is that the fight against Islamist extremism will take at least a generation to end. Islamic State, specifically, and Islamist extremism, generally, will continue to spread in the short-to-medium term. Governments, therefore, need to prepare their populations for the long haul. Several reasons account for the fact that there will be no quick end to jihadi terrorism.

Under-estimating Islamic State

The international community keeps under-estimating the Islamic State phenomenon. Following their loss of Tikrit, Kobane and Sinjar Mountain the obituary of the Islamists were written by policy makers - only for them to emerge and capture other towns like Ramadi and Palmyra. By May 2015, the Pentagon estimated that their aerial bombardment of the jihadist positions resulted in over 12,000 IS fighters killed and 10,000 fighting positions destroyed[433]. Yet the group still managed to effectively increase their territory under control. As a result, estimates of IS fighters kept being revised upwards. The CIA initially set the number of IS fighters at 20,000 then 31,000 then 50,000. The Russian security services, on the other hand, put the figure at 70,000 whilst some analysts go as far as 200,000 fighters if one considers the Sunni tribal fighters allied to Islamic State[434]. This numerical under-estimation of IS fighters also point to intelligence failures on the part of the international community. Satellite imagery and the like can also provide so much of information. Ultimately what is needed is human intelligence assets within Islamic State.

IS fighters in Iraq and Syria are further augmented by large numbers of foreign fighters, we have demonstrated in earlier chapters, who join on account of their ideological affinity.

Stalled Islamic Reformation

Whilst much can be done in terms of the 'doctrinal overhaul' called for by Ebrahim Moosa and other Islamic scholars to begin an Islamic reformation, the reality is that this will take time. There will also be resistance from more conservative Muslim ulema or clerics to such theological changes. Muslim political elites meanwhile draw political legitimacy from a conservative reading of Islamic text and they, too, will resist, any doctrinal overhaul which may challenge their political position. It should be noted that during the Reformation in Europe, there were monarchs who supported the Martin Luthers' and John Calvins' and the resultant doctrinal overhaul of Christianity. Political elites in Muslim countries are remarkably silent on these pressing issues. Note their silence even when it came to Pakistani teenager, and Nobel Peace Prize winner, Malala Yousufzai's campaign to educate Muslim women, Muslim political leadership has been lacking. It is the West which has feted Yousufzai and supported her campaign for access to education. The silence from Muslim countries, in contrast, has been deafening. The fact that there are 27000 terrorist attacks globally since 9/11 (or more than 5 per day) linked to radical Islam clearly demonstrates that radical Islam is on the ascendancy[435].In the short-to medium-term then, the popular appeal of Islamist rhetoric, as evinced in various polls alluded to in Chapter 3, will continue to draw fresh recruits to replenish Islamic State's ranks.

Under-resourced security forces

In the United Kingdom this popular appeal of the jihadi cause is seen in the dozens of families appealing to the police to stop family members from traveling to Syria to join IS. It is also seen by the fact that Britain made 218 terror-related arrests in the first 10 months of 2014. Over the same period, 100 pieces of extremist material were removed from the internet each week by British authorities[436]. As a result, British Metropolitan Assistant Police Commissioner Mark Rowley indicated that police forces were "stretched" by the "exceptionally high" number of terrorism-related investigations related to Islamist extremism[437]. This, in turn, raises the issue of inadequate funding for counter-terrorism operations at a time when Western governments are increasingly adopting austerity measures. Whilst the Islamist threat is growing exponentially, then, security forces are not properly resourced to take on the enormity of the threat posed.

Given the magnitude of the terrorist threat posed, given the finite nature of resources under the auspices of the state, it emphasizes once more the need for partnerships to develop between state and non-state actors like non-governmental organizations and multi-national corporations, as outlined in the previous chapter, to collectively confront the terrorist threat posed. This, however, will not be easy to operationalize as governments, and especially their security services, behave like feudal lords, jealously protecting their perceived fiefdom from encroachment by non-state actors.

The Failure of Political Imagination

At the end of October 2015, delegates from 17 countries as well as representatives of the European Union and the United Nations met in the Austrian capital of Vienna to discuss ways to diplomatically end the civil war in Syria[438]. After seven hours of negotiations, various aspects of a possible diplomatic solution emerged. These included, a nation-wide ceasefire between rebels and the Syrian Armed Forces but excluding IS, the re-writing of the country's constitution, a transitional government put in place and elections to be monitored by the UN[439].

Needless to say this hardly constituted a workable agreement. Assad was not in Vienna and it is unclear if he would abide by these terms. It is not clear as to his role in the transitional period or in its immediate aftermath.

Assad's allies – Moscow and Tehran – see a role for him; Washington, Riyadh and other Sunni Gulf States see no role for him; the European Union meanwhile seems ambivalent on this issue. The Syrian opposition is quite clear as to their position. They have threatened to boycott any political process which includes Assad. This aside, the biggest failure of these Vienna talks is the failure of political imagination on the part of the delegates. They have re-affirmed Syria's territorial integrity and sovereignty – refusing to recognize that Syria is already broken into Sunni, Alawite and Kurdish parts. More importantly, as was explained in an earlier chapter Islamic State cannot be defeated unless one gets buy-in from Kurds and Sunnis. These, however, will not support any political process which does not guarantee them their own state. The Vienna process, therefore, has served once again to undermine any collective effort to end IS' reign of terror.

Islamic State's Organizational Structure

More than just numbers, the IS organizational structure touched on in the opening chapter also contributes to its resilience under intense pressure. The wilayat decentralized structure adopted by IS grants the organization tremendous flexibility. Taxes are collected, services provided, forces mustered and attack plans conceived are all done at the wilayat or local level. What this means in practice is that whilst the wilayat in Samarra may be under siege by coalition forces and have to engage in defensive operations, the wilayat in Palmyra may be capable of launching offensive operations and effectively expand the territory under their control[440]. From this perspective, it is erroneous to conclude that that one is winning the battle against IS on the basis of the capture of this or that town.

In the same vein, it is wrong to assume that IS will be defeated by the death of Al-Baghdadi or military reversals in Iraq and Syria which would lead to the capture of their *de facto* capital Raqqa. For reasons outlined in earlier chapters, Islamic State, and more importantly the ideas of Islamic State will endure since it is shared by a vast swathe of Muslim public opinion. In September 2015, the Institute for the Study of War issued an important report that IS has expanded its operations globally – having established 17 affiliates in 17 African and Middle Eastern countries[441]. These affiliates include Afghanistan's Junallah, Pakistan's Terek-e-Khilafat and Jamaat al-Arhrar, Egypt's Ansar Beit al-Maqdis, Algeria's Soldiers of the Caliphate, Libya's Islamic Youth Shura, the Philippines' Abu Sayyaf, Gaza's Beit al-Maqdis, Lebanon's Free Sunnis of Baalbek Brigade, Jordan's Sons of the Call for Tawhid and Jihad, Indonesia's Ashorut Tauhid and Nigeria's Boko Haram[442]. The franchise structure of IS, then, also facilitates its growth. The oath of allegiances taken by whole regional franchises has further encouraged IS. In My 2015, it put out a video which featured Taymullah al-Somali, a Somali-born Dutch national and appealed to the militant Al Shabaab Islamists in the Horn of Africa to re-align itself with them from Al Qaeda. This marked a change on the part of Islamic State's recruitment drive. In the past, it appealed to individuals to join it, now it was appealing to whole organizations to join its cause[443].

The unfortunate truth is that Islamic State is strengthening globally and that the various al-Qaeda affiliates which have now defected to IS will further consolidate its power. Commenting on the dangers this poses to global security, Abdel Bari Atwan states,

"Numerous former al-Qaeda affiliates have shifted their allegiance to Islamic State, meaning that they have a wide-ranging geographic network – from the Caucasus to Somalia – upon which to build. Regional instability produces the security vacuum in which jihadi groups flourish. There are currently seven civil wars in progress in Muslim countries – in Iraq, Syria, Afghanistan, Libya, Yemen, Somalia and northern Nigeria – and in each country IS is active and growing in strength. Egypt, too is in danger of descending into chaos. ......The nightmare scenario would see all the major jihadi groups uniting under the IS umbrella and sectarian violence escalating into region-wide war"[444].

Neither is Islamic State's growth confined to Muslim-majority countries. Robert Maginnis, a retired senior Army officer and currently counter-insurgency scholar also noted that the battlefield could well expand into Western Europe, *"... ISIS could soon have a robust terrorist capability in Western Europe because of ISIS –trained fighters who infiltrated the flow of Mideast refugees flooding the continent"*[445]. Even without the flood of Mideast refugees however, the situation in the West is dire. Between July 2014 and August 2015, there were 32 Islamic State plots targeting the West. They spanned 10 Western countries and involved 58 individuals from 14 separate nationalities. Most worrisome, is that 29 percent of the individuals involved in the terrorist plots were converts to Islam[446].

In the opening chapter it was noted that Islamic State has established sleeper cells in 60 countries around the world. These are loosely organized with little central command and control. Members of such sleeper cells are well-trained and lead normal lives in their host countries. For these reasons, they are difficult to detect. Indeed, detection is only possible in the short-window when they are activated and begin scouting their targets. In the unlikely event, they are detected and arrested and even if all members of a particular cell are then exposed, only members of that cell are compromised. It does not compromise the other cells in the host country[447].

Even if IS loses battles in the Middle East and cedes territory in Iraq and Syria, then, it can still engage in terrorist activities through its affiliates and sleeper cells. Indeed, this is already happening. British Home Secretary Theresa May noted how British security services have foiled several such terror plots to, amongst others, assassinate an ambassador, bring down an airline and attack the stock exchange[448]. The 31 October 2015 downing of a Russian passenger flight from the Egyptian resort of Sharm-el-Sheikh which IS has claimed responsibility for also follows this trajectory[449]. The November 2015 Paris attacks as well as the double suicide bombing in southern Beirut in a Shia suburb[450] as revenge for French and Hezbollah against IS in Syria also demonstrates that while IS terrorism capabilities and global reach is on the increase.

Increasing Polarization

Such attacks, meanwhile, as explained in Chapter 2 will fuel the flames of Islamophobia which would work to the advantage of IS. The forces of Islamophobia such as PEGIDA have been sweeping across much of Europe. In the United States meanwhile, Islamophobia is growing. In May 2015, hundreds of protestors gathered outside the Islamic Community Centre of Phoenix in Arizona where they berated Islam and Prophet Muhammed[451]. All this serves to erode Western (and, indeed universal) values of tolerance and pluralism and further reinforcing the narrative of IS who divides the world between Muslims (*Dar al Islam or Place of Peace*) and the proverbial other (*Dar al Harb or Place of War*)[452] and that these are in perpetual conflict.

Polarization as explained in Chapter 2 forms an integral part of the militant's *modus operandi*. Such attempts of polarization is nothing new and has formed part of the repertoire of revolutionaries for at least two generations. It was in the 1960s that Brazilian revolutionary Carlos Marighella, also known as the "*father of modern terrorism*" penned his infamous *Minimanual of the Urban Guerrilla*[453]. In it he spoke of the need to escalate violence, compelling security forces to become more repressive. In the process the "soft centre" (the forces of moderation) are eliminated and greater polarization will result. This seems to be working quite well not only in Europe and the United States but also in the Middle East. In Iraq, Shi'a militias and Iranian Revolutionary Guards Corps attached to the Iraqi army, as explained above, have wreaked havoc on Sunni areas liberated from IS control. A similar dynamic is taking place in Syria – further exacerbated by the alliance between Moscow, Tehran and the minority Alawite regime in Damascus. In the process, this has served not only to exacerbate sectarian tensions but have also served to radicalize these Sunnis – increasing recruits into IS. Recognizing the fact that polarization in the context of the West and the Middle East only serves the strengthen the IS narrative and encourages further radicalization and therefore recruitment, it would be easy to recommend that to counteract the narrative of IS, governments and peoples around the world have to strengthen the "soft centre" – the forces of moderation, tolerance and peaceful co-existence. In this way, too, one strengthens resilience against radicalization. The security forces, meanwhile, have to exercise restraint clearly separating combatants from non-combatants and making clear that just because a Sunni community may share they share the same faith as members of IS does not make them the enemy.

This, however, is not as easy as it sounds. Politicians are swayed by votes – including those votes by popular jingoistic sentiments of your PEGIDAs. Under the circumstances, one should not be surprised that right-wing politicians like Geert Wilders in the Netherlands or Donald Trump in the United States have played the anti-Islam card so deftly. Similarly, do not expect Shi'a militias in Iraq and Syria not to seek retribution against innocent Sunnis for the atrocities committed by their co-religionists in Islamic State. There is no conception of the national interest in the Middle East where states have always been characterised by a multiplicity of sectarian interests. Under the circumstances, polarisation will grow. Recruitment into IS will intensify as the jihadists directly benefit from feelings of alienation, contempt of the status quo, suspicion and hatred.

The Toxic Mix of Demographics and Environmental Variables

Certain demographic and environmental variables exacerbate religious conflicts which also works to the advantage of groups like Islamic State. The potential for future conflict along religious lines is a distinct possibility given certain demographic trends. According to the Pew Research Centre, Islam will grow faster than any other religion over the next four decades. To put it differently, the number of Muslims will grow by a staggering 73 percent between 2010 and 2050[454]. Whilst the rise of the number of Muslims does not necessarily mean more conflict since the majority of Muslims do not subscribe to the austere Salafi takfiri brand of Islam which IS represents, the reality is that in societies with a history of sectarian strife (think here of India with ongoing tensions between Hindus and Muslims) or where there are scarcity of resources (think here of the Sahel) societies will divide along sectarian (ethnic and religious) lines in order to compete for such scarce resources. The city of Jos in Nigeria, for instance has, witnessed ethno-religious conflict since 2001 which has pitted Christian Berom against Muslim Hausas. At the heart of the conflict is access to fertile land at a time when the population is growing whilst the arable land has been under sustained threat due to the ongoing drought[455].

Another dimension of the demographic problem is highlighted by Eric Kaufmann in his seminal book Shall the Religious Inherit the Earth? Demography and Politics in the Twenty-First Century[456]. He convincingly argued that the fertility rates among non-religious communities is displaying the lowest fertility rates in human history – often less than one child per woman. Conversely, the fertility rates of deeply religious people are several times this. Moreover this holds true across faith communities – Buddhist, Christian, Hindu, Muslim, or Jew. This is unsurprising given the fact that religious communities emphasize traditional roles for women and all three Abrahamic faiths encourage their adherents to 'go forth and multiply'[457]. This growing population amongst the religious will, according to Kaufmann see greater conflict between the religious and secular polities as we witnessed contestation around abortion and the teaching of creationism vs evolution in schools in the West. In largely Muslim societies we witness the assassination of writers promoting secularism as well as the incarceration of liberal bloggers as in Saudi Arabia. This demographic trend would also see greater conflict between different religious fundamentalisms. In Israel, for instance it is religious Jews who are settlers in the occupied West Bank and who keep attempting to expand the borders of the Palestinian state. In Myanmar, we have watched Buddhists brutally attack minority Rohingya Muslims. In Egypt Sunni Muslims have attacked Coptic Christians and Shi'a Muslims. This adds to polarization between communities and provides further fuel to the growth of Islamic State.

In conclusion, then, problems surrounding under-estimating IS, a doctrinal overhaul of Islam, the decentralized wilayat structure of IS, its global spread via affiliate organizations, civil wars in Muslim countries, under-resourced security forces, growing polarization and sectarian strife between and within societies as well as demographic and environmental variables all work to the advantage of Islamic State in particular and religious fundamentalism generally. Despite the various policy prescriptions aimed at mitigating the forces of militant jihadism, I believe that the world is headed towards a global confrontation between the forces of liberal democracy and those of Islamist extremism. Al-Baghdadi will have his Armageddon.

¹ Raymond Ibrahim, "The CIA Doesn't Know Why Muslims Join IS," PJ Media. 18 March 2015. Internet: http://www.meforum.org/5138/cia-muslims-IS. Date accessed: 4 June 2015.
² Hussein Solomon, "South Africa and the Islamic State," RIMA Occasional Papers Vol. 3 No. 3, April 2015, p. 2. Internet: http://muslimsinafrica.wordpress.com/2015/04/09/south-africa-and-the-islamic-state-professor-hussein-solomon. Date accessed: 21 April 2015.
³ Michael R. Gordon and Eric Schmitt, "Iran Still Aids Terrorism and Bolsters Syria's President, State Department Finds," The New York Times. 19 June 2015. Internet: http://nytimes.com/2015/06/20/world/middleeast/state-department-terrorism-report-iran. Date accessed: 1 July 2015.
⁴ADF, "IS moves into Africa," Defence Web. 29 July 2015. Internet: http://www.defenceweb.co.za/index.[hp?option=com_content&view=article&id=401. Date accessed: 3 August 2015.
⁵Aymenn Jawad Al-Tamimi, "The Evolution in Islamic State Administration: The Documentary Evidence," Rubin Centre. 6 August 2015. Internet: http://www.rubincenter.org/2015/08/the-evolution-in-islamic-state-administration-the. Date accessed: 17 August 2015.
⁶*Ibid.*
⁷*Ibid.*
⁸*Ibid.*
⁹*Ibid.*
¹⁰Michael Weiss and Hassan Hassan, ISIS: Inside the Army of Terror. Regan Arts. New York. 2015, p. 1.
¹¹Abdel Bari Atwan, "When it comes to `Islamic State,' the West just doesn't get it," Open Democracy, 9 July 2015. Internet: https://www.opendemocracy.net/arab-awakening/abdel-bari-atwan/when-it-comes-to. Date accessed: 14 September 2015.
¹²Aymenn Jawad Al-Tamimi, "The Evolution in Islamic State Administration: The Documentary Evidence," *op. cit.*
¹³Anne Barnard and Time Arango, "Using Violence and Persuasion, IS Makes Political Gains," The New York Times. 3 June 2015. Internet: http://www.nytimes.com/2015/06/04/world/IS-making-political-gains-.html. Date accessed: 4 June 2015.
¹⁴ADF, "IS moves into Africa," *op. cit.*
¹⁵*Ibid.*
¹⁶*Ibid.*
¹⁷Michael Weiss and Hassan Hassan, ISIS: Inside the Army of Terror, *op.*

cit., p. 118.

[18] ADF, "IS moves into Africa," *op. cit.*

[19] Michael Weiss and Hassan Hassan, ISIS: Inside the Army of Terror, *op. cit.*, 119.

[20] Aymenn Jawad Al-Tamimi, "The Evolution in Islamic State Administration: The Documentary Evidence," *op. cit.*

[21] ADF, "IS moves into Africa," *op. cit.*

[22] Andrew Phillips, "The Islamic State's challenge to international order," Australian Journal of International Affairs. 2014. Internet: http://dx.doi.org/10.1080/10357718.2014.947355. Date accessed: 26 October 2015, p. 2.

[23] Aymenn Jawad Al-Tamimi, "The Evolution in Islamic State Administration: The Documentary Evidence," *op. cit.* It should be noted that Jabhat al-Nusra was to remain aligned to Al Qaeda central even though its origins lay with Al-Baghdadi and the Islamic State. We will shortly see how Jabhat al-Nusra was to become a rival to Islamic State in Syria.

[24] ADF, "IS moves into Africa," *op. cit.*

[25] *Ibid.*

[26] Michael Weiss and Hassan Hassan, ISIS: Inside the Army of Terror, *op. cit.*, p. 120.

[27] ADF, "IS moves into Africa," *op. cit.*

[28] Abdel Bari Atwan, "When it comes to `Islamic State,' the West just doesn't get it," *op. cit.*

[29] Andrew Phillips, "The Islamic State's challenge to international order," *op. cit.*, p. 2.

[30] Nima Elbagir, Paul Cruickshank and Mohammed Tawfeeq, "Boko Haram purportedly pledges allegiance to IS," CNN. 9 March 2015. Internet: edition.cnn.com/2015/03/07/Africa-region-boko-haram-IS. Date accessed: 10 March 2015.

[31] Hussein Solomon, "Expanding the Jihad: IS in Africa," RIMA Occasional Papers Vol. 3 No. 2, March 2015, p. 2. Internet: https://muslimsinafrica.wordpress.com/2015/03/11/expanding-the-jihad-IS-in-africa-professor-hussein-solomon/. Date accessed: 21 April 2015.

[32] Elizabeth Whitman, "Islamic State recruitment: IS Seeks Fighters From Caucasus, Central Asia and Indonesia," IB Times. 13 August 2015. Internet: www.ibtimes.com/islamic-state-recruitment-IS-seeks-fighters-caucasus-central. Date accessed: 17 August 2015.

[33] *Ibid.*

[34] *Ibid.*

[35] "Splinter groups breaks from al Qaeda in North Africa," Reuters. 15 September 2014. Internet: www.reuters.com. Date accessed: 15 September 2014.

36 ADF, "IS moves into Africa," *op. cit.*
37 Mordechai Kedar, "IS will try for Tunisia next," Breaking Israel News. 8 October 2014. Internet: http://www.breakingisraelnews.com/22627/IS-will-try-tunisia-next. Date accessed: 13 October 2014.
38 Hassan M. Abukar, "Is IS aligned to or influencing African Jihadi Groups?" African Arguments. 28 October 2014. Internet: http://africanarguments.org/2014/10/28/is-IS-allied-to-or-influencing-african-jihadi-groups-by-hassan-m-abukar. Date accessed: 10 March 2015.
39 Simon Tomlinson, "IS opens new front in North Africa after two extremist groups in Libya and Egypt pledge allegiance to its terror chief," Mail Online 2 December 2014. Internet: www.dailymail.co.uk/news/articlee2853255/IS-opens-new-extremist-groups-Libya-Egypt-pledge-allegiance-terror-leader.html. Date accessed: 10 March 2015.
40 "Israeli general: Hamas aiding IS affiliate in Sinai," Britain Israel Communications and Research Centre. 3 July 2015. Internet: http://www.bicom.org.uk/news-article/26004. Date accessed: 7 July 2015.
41 *Ibid.*
42 *Ibid.*
43 "Islamic State threatens Israel in new videos," IBN News. 20 October 2015. Internet: http://www.ibnlive.com/news/world/islamic-state-threatens-israel-in-new-videos. Date accessed: 26 October. 2015.
44 *Ibid.*
45 Ariel Ben Solomon, "ISIS trying to hijack Palestinian jihad as its own," Jerusalem Post. 22 October 2015. Internet: http://www.jpost.com/Arab-Israeli--Conflict/isis-trying-to-hijack-Palestinian-jihad-as-its-own. Date accessed: 26 October 2015.
46 *Ibid.*
47 Elbagir, Cruickshank and Tawfeeq, *op. cit.*
48 Abdel Bari Atwan, "When it comes to 'Islamic State,' the west just doesn't get it," *op. cit.*
49 Harriet Alexander and Alastair Beach, "How ISIL is funded, trained and operating in Iraq and Syria," The Telegraph. 23 August 2014. Internet: http://www.telegraph.co.uk/news/worldnews/middleeast/iraq/11052919/How-Isil-is-funded-trained-and-operating-in-Iraq-and-Syria.html. Date accessed: 20 November 2014.
50 Abdel Bari Atwan, "When it comes to 'Islamic State,' the west just doesn't get it," *op. cit.*
51 Hussein Solomon, "IS in Africa: The Danger of Political Correctness," RIMA Occasional Papers. Vol. 2 No. 11, October 2014, p. 1. Internet: https://muslimsinafrica.wordpress.com/2014/10/13/isis-in-africa-the-danger-of-political-correctness-professor-hussein-solomon. Date accessed:

6 November 2015.
⁵²Jacob Zenn, "Wilayat West Africa Reboots for the Caliphate," CTC Sentinel. Vol. 8, Issue 8, August 2015. Internet: https://www.ctc.usma.edu/posts/wilayat-west-africa-reboots-for-the-caliphate. Date accessed: 15 September 2015.
⁵³*Ibid.*
⁵⁴ Elbagir, Cruickshank and Tawfeeq, *op. cit.*
⁵⁵John W. Williams, "Carlos Marighela: The father of urban guerrilla warfare," Studies in Conflict and Terrorism, Vol. 12 No.1, 1989, pp. 1-20.
⁵⁶ David von Drehle, "The European Front," Time, 26 January 2015, p. 18.
⁵⁷Arno Tausch, "Estimates on the Global Threat of Islamic State Terrorism in the Face of the 2015 Paris and Copenhagen Attacks," Rubin Center. 13 July 2015. Internet: http://www.rubin.center.org/2015/07/estimates-on-the-global-threat-of-islamic-state-terrorism. Date accessed: 29 July 2015.
⁵⁸ Lizzie Deardon, "Germany anti-Islam protests: Biggest Pegida march ever in Dresden as rest of Germany shows disgust with lights-out," The Independent. 5 January 2015. Internet: http://www.independent.co-uk/news/world/europe/germany-antiislam-protests-biggest-pegida-march-ever-in-dresden-as-rest-of-germany-shows-disgust. Date accessed: 21 April 2015.
⁵⁹Daniel Pipes, "Why the Paris massacre will have Limited Impact," National Review Online. 14 November 2015. Internet: http://www.meforum.org/5628/paris-massacre-impact. Date accessed: 15 November 2015.
⁶⁰Tausch, *op. cit.*, p. 4.
⁶¹ David von Drehle, "The European Front," Time, 26 January 2015, pp. 18-19.
⁶²Aaron Brown, "'Just wait…' Islamic state reveals it has smuggled thousands of extremists into Europe," Daily Express. 10 September 2015. Internet: http://www.express.co.uk/news/world/55434/Islamic-State-ISIS-Smuggler-Thousands-Extremists-into-Europe-Refugees. Date accessed: 14 September 2015.
⁶³Daniel Pipes, "IS Attacks on the West," The Washington Times. 22 May 2015. Internet: http://www.meforum.org/5255/IS-attacks-the-west. Date accessed: 4 June 2015.
⁶⁴Alessandria Masi, "ISIS, aka Islamic State, Warns of Sleeper Cells Attacks on US interests in retaliation for Bombings," IB Times. 8 August 2015. Internet: http://www.ibtimes.com/isis-aka-islamic-state-warns-sleeper-cell-attacks-us-interests-retaliation-bombings-1653476. Date accessed: 1 December 2015.
⁶⁵ Kareem Abdul-Jabbar, "Paris Was Not About Religion," Time, 26 January 2015.

⁶⁶Daniel Pipes, "IS Attacks on the West," *op. cit.*
⁶⁷*Ibid.*
⁶⁸Brian Bennett, "FBI directors says Islamic State poses greater threat to U.S. than Al Qaeda," LA Times. 22 July 2015. Internet: http://www.latimes.com/nation/la-na-fbi-comey20150722-story.html. Date accessed: 28 July 2015.
⁶⁹ Gordon and Schmitt, *op. cit.*
⁷⁰*Ibid.*
⁷¹Ben Hubbard, "Offering services, IS Digs in Deeper in Seized Territories," The New York Times. 16 June 2015. Internet: http://www.nytimes.com/2015/06/17/world/middleeast/offering-services-IS-ensconces-itself. Date accessed: 17 June 2015.
⁷²Aymenn Jawad Al-Tamimi, "The Evolution in Islamic State Administration: The Documentary Evidence," *op. cit.*
⁷³Anne Barnard and Tim Arango, "Using Violence and Persuasion, IS Makes Political Gains," *op. cit.*
⁷⁴Michael Weiss and Hassan Hassan, ISIS: Inside the Army of Terror, *op. cit.*, p. 207.
⁷⁵*Ibid.*, p. 200.
⁷⁶*Ibid.*, p. 207.
⁷⁷*Ibid.*, pp. 205-206
⁷⁸Abdel Bari Atwan, "When it comes to 'Islamic State,' the West just doesn't get it," *op. cit.*
⁷⁹*Ibid.*
⁸⁰ADF, "Feature: IS moves into Africa," Defence Web. 29 July 2015. Internet: http://www.defenceweb.co.za/index.php?option=com_content&view=article&id=401. Date accessed: 3 August 2015.
⁸¹Ben Hubbard, "Offering services, IS Digs in Deeper in Seized Territories," *op. cit.*
⁸²ADF, "IS moves into Africa," *op.cit.*
⁸³ John Hall, "'IS controls as many as 90,000 Twitter accounts which it uses to spread sick propaganda and radicalise Westerners, terror experts reveal," Mail Online. 6 March 2015. Internet: www.dailymail.co.uk/news/article-2982673/IS-controls-90000-twitter-accounts-which-it-uses-to-spread-sick-propaganda-and-radicalise-westerners-terror-experts-reveal.html. Date accessed: 10 July 2015.
⁸⁴Brian Bennett, "FBI director says Islamic State poses greater threat to U.S. than Al Qaeda," *op.cit.*
⁸⁵Michael Weiss and Hassan Hassan, ISIS: Inside the Army of Terror, *op. cit.*, p. 173.
⁸⁶*Ibid.*, p. 170.

[87] Quoted in Jessica Stern and J.M. Berger, ISIS: The State of Terror. William Collins. London. 2015, p. 147.
[88] ADF, "IS moves into Africa," *op. cit.*
[89] "The Islamic State: The propaganda war," The Economist, 15 August 2015. Internet: http://www.economist.come/news/middle-east-and-africa/21660989-terrorists-vicious. Date accessed: 17 August 2015.
[90] *Ibid.*
[91] *Ibid.*
[92] Elizabeth Whitman, "Islamic State Recruitment: IS Seeks Fighters from Caucasus, Central Asia and Indonesia," *op. cit.*
[93] Gordon and Schmitt, *op. cit.*
[94] Elizabeth Whitman, "Islamic State Recruitment: IS Seeks Fighters from Caucasus, Central Asia and Indonesia," *op. cit.*
[95] Emine Saner, "Mundane reality of martyrs," Mail and Guardian, 31 July – 6 August 2015, Vol. 31 No. 31, p. 16.
[96] ADF, "IS moves into Africa," *op. cit.*
[97] *Ibid.*
[98] Abdel Bari Atwan, "When it comes to `Islamic State,' the West just doesn't get it," *op. cit.*
[99] Paul Tilsley, "South Africa increasingly seen as key ISIS pipeline for jihadis, cash," Fox News. 3 October 2015. Internet: http://www.foxnews.com/world/2015/10/03/south-africa-increasingly-isis-pipeline-for-jihadis-cash. Date accessed: 10 October 2015.
[100] Quoted in Hussein Solomon, "South Africa and the Islamic State," *op. cit.*, p. 1.
[101] Tilsley, *op. cit.*
[102] "Nigeria `blocks recruitment' by Islamic State," Starr FM Online. 11 August 2015. Internet: http://starrfmonline.com/1.5908766. Date accessed: 12 August 2015.
[103] *Ibid.*
[104] *Ibid.*
[105] Colin Freeman and Hassan Morajea, "Tunisia-Gunman: The gunman who loved Facebook and Real Madrid," The Sunday Telegraph. London. 28 June 2015, p. 2.
[106] "The Islamic State group on Saturday claimed responsibility for a massacre in a Tunisian seaside resort that killed nearly 40 people, most of them British tourists, in the worst attack in the country's recent history," France24.com. Internet: http://www.france24.com/en/20150627-is-group-tunisia-massacre-sousse. Date accessed: 1 July 2015.
[107] Colin Freeman and Hassan Morajea, *op.cit.*
[108] *Ibid.*

[109] Alessandra Bruno, "Tunisia's Terrorism Problem Goes Beyond Islamic State," Geopolitical Monitor. 14 July 2015. Internet: http://geopoliticalmonitor.com/tunisias-terrorism-problem-beyond-islamic-state. Date accessed: 15 July 2015.

[110] Daniel Cohen and Danielle Levin, "How IS Gained Traction in the Middle East," Forbes. 10 August 2015. Internet: http://www.forbes.com/sites/realspin/2015/08/10/how-IS-gained-traction-in-the-middle-east. Date accessed: 12 August 2015.

[111] Al Jazeera Centre for Studies, "Tunisia's security crIS and government's inability to cope," AMEC Insights. Briefing No. 13/2015. 27 July 2015p. p. 2.

[112] Tarek Fatah, "Face Reality: Many Muslims Support IS," The Toronto Sun. 16 Jun2 2015. Internet: http://www.meforum.org/5331/many-muslims-support-IS. Date accessed: 17 June 2015.

[113] *Ibid.*

[114] Von Drehle, *op. cit.*, p. 18.

[115] Kimiko de Freyas-Tamura, "Junaid Hussain, IS Recruiter, Reported Killed in Airstrike," The New York Times. 27 August 2015. Internet: http://www.nytimes.com/2015/08/28/world/middleeast/junaid-hussain-islamic-state-recruiter. Date accessed: 31 August 2015.

[116] Abdel Bari Atwan, "When it comes to `Islamic State,' the West just doesn't get it," *op. cit.*

[117] Abukar, *op. cit.*

[118] Kareem Abdul-Jabbar, "Paris Was Not About Religion," Time, 26 January 2015, p. 15.

[119] Scott Bronstein and Drew Griffin, "Self-funded and deep-rooted: How ISIS makes its millions," CNN. 7 October 2014. Internet: http://edition.cnn.com/2014/10/06/world/meast/isis-funding. Date accessed: 26 November 2014.

[120] "Islamic State Group Now Controls Key Drug Trafficking Routes," teleSUR. 30 July 2015. Internet: http://www.telesur.tv.net/english/news/Islamic-State-Group-Now-Controls-Key-Drug-Trafficking. Date accessed: 19 September 2015.

[121] *Ibid.*

[122] *Ibid.*

[123] Sarah Almukhtar, "IS Finances are Strong," New York Times. 19 May 2015. Internet: http://www.nytimes.com/interactive/2015/05/19/world/middleeast/IS-finances.html. Date accessed: 2 June 2015.

[124] Aymenn Jawad Al-Tamimi, "The Evolution in Islamic State Administration: The Documentary Evidence," *op. cit.*

[125] Ben Hubbard, "IS Appears to Destroy 2 Palmyra Tombs, Flaunting

Wreckage in Photos," The New York Times. 24 June 2015. Internet: http://www.nytimes.com/2015/05/25/world/middleeast/islamic-state-IS-destroys-palmyra. Date accessed: 1 July 2015.
[126]ADF, "IS moves into Africa," *op. cit.*
[127]*Ibid.*
[128] Von Drehle, *op. cit.*, p. 18.
[129]Scott Bronstein and Drew Griffin, "Self-funded and deep-rooted: How ISIS makes its millions, *op. cit.*
[130]*Ibid.*
[131]Harriet Alexander and Alastair Beach, "How ISIL is funded, trained and operating in Iraq and Syria," The Telegraph. 23 August 2014. Internet: http://www.telegraph.co.uk/news/worldnews/middleeast/iraq/11052919/How-Isil-is-funded-trained-and-operating-in-Iraq-and-Syria.html. Date accessed: 20 November 2014.
[132]"ISIS Got Up to $45 million in Ransoms in Past Year, UN Says," Time Magazine. Internet: http://time.com/3605061/isis-ransom-united-nations. Date accessed: 26 November 2014.
[133] Scott Bronstein and Drew Griffin, "Self –funded and deep-rooted: How ISIS makes its millions," *op. cit.*
[134]John Defterios, "ISIS: Can coalition cut off funding of world's wealthiest terror group?" CNN. 27 October 2014. Internet: http://edition.cnn.com/2014/10/27/business/isis-wealthiest-terror-group-defterios/iref=obnetwork. Date accessed: 26 November 2014.
[135]Tilsley, *op. cit.*
[136]Nabeelah Shaikh, "Focus on ISIS is R78m airport probe," Independent Online. 20 September 2015. Internent: http://mobi.iol.co.za/#!/focus-on-isis-in-r78m-airport-probe-1.918566. Date accessed: 28 September 2015.
[137]Aymenn Jawad Al-Tamimi, "The Evolution in Islamic State Administration: The Documentary Evidence," *op. cit.*
[138]Almukhtar, *op. cit.*
[139]Michael Weiss and Hassan Hassan, ISIS: Inside the Army of Terror, *op. cit.*, p. 124.
[140]*Ibid.*, p. 126.
[141]*Ibid.*, pp. 128-129.
[142]Harriet Alexander and Alastair Beach, "How ISIL is funded, trained and operating in Iraq and Syria," *op. cit.*
[143]Tim Arango and Anne Barnard, "With Victories, IS Dispels Hope of a Swift Decline," The New York Times, 23 May 2015. Internet: http://nytimes.com/2015/05/24/world/middleeast/with-victories-IS-dispels-hope-of-a-swift-decline.html. Date accessed: 2 June 2015.
[144]*Ibid.*
[145]*Ibid.*

¹⁴⁶*Ibid.*
¹⁴⁷*Ibid.*
¹⁴⁸*Ibid.*
¹⁴⁹*Ibid.*
¹⁵⁰*Ibid.*
¹⁵¹Jonathan Spyer, "Dispatch from Iraq: Iran-Backed Militias Keep IS at Bay, for a Price," The Australian. 4 July 2015. Internet: http://www.meforum.org/5365/iraq-iran-militia-IS. Date accessed: 8 July 2015.
¹⁵²Tim Arango, "IS Suicide Attack Kills 2 Iraqi Generals Near Ramadi," The New York Times, 27 August 2015. Internet: http://www.nytimes.com/2015/08/28/world/middleeast/iraq-IS-suicide-attack-ramadi.html. Date accessed: 31 August 2015.
¹⁵³*Ibid.*
¹⁵⁴ Libya profile – Timeline, BBC. 27 May 2015. Internet: http://www.bbc.com/news/world-africa-13766445. Date accessed: 2 June 2015.
¹⁵⁵*Ibid.*
¹⁵⁶Suliman Ali Zway and David D. Kirkpatrick, Western officials alarmed as IS expands territory in Libya, New York Times, 31 May 2015. Internet: http://www.nytimes.com/2015/06/01/world/africa/western-officials-alarmed-as-islamic-state-expands-territory-in-libya.html. Date accessed: 2 June 2015.
¹⁵⁷"Suicide bombing claimed by Islamic State in western Libyan city kills five: official," Reuters, 31 May 2015. Internet: http://www.reuters.com/article/2015/05/31/us-libya-security-idUSKBN0OG09220150531. Date accessed: 2 June 2015.
¹⁵⁸Zway and Kirkpatrick, *op. cit.*
¹⁵⁹"Libya fears Iraq-like IS scenario," News 24.com. 2 June 2015. Internet: http://www.news24.com/Africa/News/Libya-fears-Iraq-like-IS-scenario-20150601. Date accessed: 2 June 2015.
¹⁶⁰Islamic state militants in Libya seize Sirte airport, BBC. 29 May 2015. Internet: http://www.bbc.com.news/world-world-africa-32935412. Date accessed: 2 June 2015.
¹⁶¹ Tomlinson, *op. cit.*
¹⁶² Simon Allison, "Think Again – too late to start worrying about the Islamic State in Africa," ISS Africa. 7 October 2014.
¹⁶³ Quoted in Michael J. Totten, "The IS of Africa," World Affairs Journal. Internet: http://worldaffairsjournal.org. Date accessed: 10 March 2015.
¹⁶⁴ Quoted in Adam Chandler, "Tunisia After the Museum Attack," The Atlantic. 1 April 2015. Internet: www.theatlantic.com/international/archive/2015/03/tunisia-in-bardos-

aftermath/389039. Date accessed: 1 April 2015.
[165] Eileen Byrne and Chris Stephen, "Tunisian and French presidents attend unity rally after Tunis museum attack, The Guardian. 29 March 2015. Internet: http://the guardian.com/world/2015/mar/29/Tunisian-french-presidents-unity-rally-tunis-museum-attack. Date accessed: 1 April 2015.
[166] Carlotta Gall, "Official Says that Commander of Group that Massacred 21 in Tunisia is Dead," The New York Times. 19 March 2015. Internet: http://www.nytimes.com/2015/03/30/world/africa/official-says-commander-of-group-that-massacred-21-in-tunisia-is-dead.html. Date accessed: 2 April 2015.
[167] "The Islamic State group on Saturday claimed responsibility for a massacre in a Tunisian seaside resort that killed nearly 40 people, most of them British tourists, in the worst attack in the country's recent history," France24.com. 27 June 2015. Date accessed: http://www.france24.com/en/20150627-is-group-tunisia-massacre-sousse. Date accessed: 1 July 2015.
[168] Jamey Keaten and Paul Schemm, "Islamic State claims responsibility for Tunisia attack," Associated Press. 30 March 2015. Internet: http://wfsb.com/story/28558893/islamic-state-claims-responsibility-for-tunisia-attack. Date accessed: 1 April 2015.
[169] Ted Thornhill, "Children's worker reveals how mother's suicide helped turn the Kouachi brothers from `sweet young boys' into infamous Islamist murderers," Mail Online. 19 January 2015. Internet: http://www.dailymail.co.uk/news/article-2916450/Chidren-s-worker-reveals-Kouachi-brother-s-sweet-young-boys-infamous-Islamists-murderers.html. Date accessed: 12 September 2015.
[170] Heather Saul, "Paris attacks timeline: From Charlie Hebdo to a Jewish grocery store – how two hostage situations unfolded," The Independent. 9 January 2015. Internet: http://www.independent.co.uk/europe/paris-attacks-timelne-from-charlie-hebdo-to-dammartinengoele-how-the-double-hostage-situation-unfolded-9968543.html. Date accessed: 12 September 2015.
[171] Angelique Chrisaftis, Charlie Hebdo attackers' born, raised and radicalized in Paris, The Guardian. 12 January 2015. Internet: http://www.theguardian.com/world/2015.jan/12-sp-charlie-hebdo-attackers-kids-france-radicalised-paris. Date accessed: 12 September 2015.
[172] Von Drehle, *op. cit.*, p. 18.
[173] *Ibid.*
[174] *Ibid.*
[175] *Ibid.*
[176] Tom Parfitt, "ISIS claims Paris attacks as Revenge for Syrian airstrikes and insulting Islam's prophet," Sunday Express. 15 November 2015.

Internet: http://www.express.co.uk/news/world/619363/Islamic-State-ISIS-Twitter-Paris-attacks. Date accessed: 15 November 2015.
[177] Bob Tayor, "Rev James V. Schall's brilliant analysis of Islam, IS, and the West," Communities Digital News. 8 October 2014. Internet: http://www.commdiginews.com/world-news-rev-james-v-schalls-brilliant-analysis-of. Date accessed: 13 October 2014.
[178] Editorial: Muslim cleric denounce IS," Parker Pioneer. 8 October 2014. Internet: http://parkerpioneer.net/opinionarticle_8898fa7e-4f35-11e4-b85b-b33c3de4faf. Date accessed: 13 October 2014.
[179]"The Islamic State: The propaganda war," The Economist, 15 August 2015, *op. cit.*
[180]Abdel Bari Atwan, "When it comes to `Islamic State,' the West just doesn't get it," *op. cit.*
[181]Aymenn Jawad Al-Tamimi, "The Evolution in Islamic State Administration: The Documentary Evidence," *op. cit.*
[182]"Islam and slavery: The persistence of history," The Economist. 22August 2015. Internet: http://www.economist.com/node/21661812. Date accessed: 24 August 2015.
[183]*Ibid.*
[184]*Ibid.*
[185]Bridget Johnson, "Saudi Cleric Who Issued Fatwa on WMD Permissibility Pledges Allegiance to IS," PJ Media. 25 August 2015. Internet: http://pjmedia.com/blog/saudi-cleric-who-issued-fatwa-on-wmd-permissibility-pledge. Date accessed: 27 August 2015.
[186] David Motadel, "The Ancestors of IS," The New York Times. 23 September 2014. Internet: http://www.nytimes.com/2014/09/24/opinion/the-ancestors-of-IS.html. Date accessed: 3 October 2014.
[187] Karen Armstrong, Islam: A Short History. The Modern Library. New York. 2000, p. 135.
[188] Quoted in Mirza Tahir Ahmad, Murder in the Name of Allah. Lutterworth Press. Cambridge. 1989, p. 21.
[189]Tarek Fatah, "Tackling Islamism, Post-Chattanooga," The Toronto Sun. 21 July 2015. Internet: http://www.meforum.org/5394/islamism-chattanooga. Date accessed: 28 July 2015.
[190]*Ibid.*
[191] Jerrold M. Post, The Mind of the Terrorist: The Psychology of Terrorism from the IRA to Al Qaeda. Palgrave Macmillan. New York. 2007, p. 175.
[192] Ahmad, *op. cit.*, p. 58.
[193] Ahmad Thomson, Dajjal: The Anti-Christ. Ta-Ha Publishers Ltd. London. 2011, pp. 2, 5, 61.

[194] *Ibid.*, p. 186.
[195] *Ibid.*, p. 187.
[196] Fernando Betancor, "Outside the box: is the Islamic State close to victory?," Open Democracy. 10 September 2015. Internet: http://www.opendemocracy.net/arab-awakening/fernando-betancor/outside-box-is-islamic. Date accessed: 15 September 2015.
[197] Jessica Stern and J.M. Berger, ISIS: The State of Terror, *op. cit.*, p. 219.
[198] EbrahimMoosa, "My madrassas classmate hated politics, then joined the Islamic State," The Morning Call. 22 August 2015. Internet: http://www.mcall.com/opinion/mc-islamic-state-recrut-0823-20150822-story.html. Date accessed: 24 August 2015.
[199] "Man from Ghana joins Islamic State, family says," News 24. 26 August 2015. Internet: http://www.news24.com/Africa/News/Man-from-Ghana-joins-Islamic-State-family-says. Date accessed: 27 August 2015.
[200] Gregory Tomlin, "IS `Mein Kampf' discovered in Pakistan; promises final solution in 2020," Christian Examiner. 18 August 2015. Internet: http://www.christian examiner.com/article/IS.mein.kampf.discovered.in.pakistan.promises. Date accessed: 20 August 2015.
[201] Dale Hurd, "ISIS's First Step: Conquer Rome, Defeat Christianity," CBN News. 1 October 2015. Internet: http://www.cbn.com/cbnnews/world/2015/October/ISISs-First-Step-Conqering-Rome. Date accessed: 5 October 2015.
[202] *Ibid.*
[203] Gregory Tomlin, "IS 'Mein Kampf' discovered in Pakistan; promises final solution in 2020," *op. cit.*
[204] Saladdin Ahmed, "Islamic State: More popular than you think," Open Democracy. 17 June 2015. Internet: https://www.opendemocracy.net/arab-awakening/saladdin=ahmed/aljazeera-poll-81-percent. Date accessed: 14 September 2015.
[205] Andrew G. Bostom, "Benghazi: From `See no Sharia' to Ansar al-Sharia," The American Thinker. 25 December 2012.
[206] James M. Dorsey, "Moroccans fans support for ISIL: Protestors of Jihadists," Hurriyet Daily News. 13 October 2014. Internet: http://hurriyetdailynews.com/moroccan-fans-support-for-isil-protests-or-jihadists. Date accessed: 13 October 2014.
[207] Tarek Fatah, "Face Reality: Many Muslims Support IS," The Toronto Sun. 16 June 2015. Internet: http://www.meforum.org/5331/many-muslims-support-IS. Date accessed: 17 June 2015.
[208] Tausch, *op. cit.*, p. 8.
[209] *Ibid.*

[210] *Ibid.*, p. 4.
[211] Tarek Fatah, "Face Reality: Many Muslims Support IS," *op. cit.*
[212] *Ibid.*
[213] "CIA says IS numbers underestimated," Al Jazeera. 12 September 2014. Internet: http://www.aljazeera.com/news/middleeast/2014/09/cia-triples-number-islamic-state-fighters-20149123291623733.html. Date accessed: 16 September 2015.
[214] Saladdin Ahmed, "Islamic State: More popular than you think," *op. cit.*
[215] Douglas Murray, "Smash IS now – we'll all pay later," The Spectator, 30 May 2015. Internet: http://www.spectator.co.uk/features/9541932/smash-IS-no2-or-well-all-pay-later. Date accessed: 3 June 2015.
[216] Aymenn Jawad Al-Tamimi, "The Evolution in Islamic State Administration," *op. cit.*
[217] Jenny Stanton, "Isis vows revenge after leader Abu Bakr al-Baghdadi is `forced to give up control after he was seriously injured in air strike,' Mail Online. 2 May 2015. Internet: http://www.dailymail.co.uk/news/article-3064951/Isis-vows-revenge-leader-Abu-Bakr-al-Baghdadi-forced-control-seriously-wounded-air-strike.html. Date accessed: 10 September 2015.
[218] Mark Mazzetti and Scott Shane, "For U.S., Killing Terrorists Is a Means to an End," the New York Times. 17 June 2015. Internet: http://www.nytimes.com/2015/06/17/world/middleeast/al-qaeda-arabian-peninsula-yemen. Date accessed: 17 June 2015.
[219] *Ibid.*
[220] *Ibid.*
[221] *Ibid.*
[222] Hussein Solomon, Jihad: A South African Perspective. Sun Media, Bloemfontein, 2013, p. 70.
[223] Jeremy McDermott, "20 Years After Pablo: The Evolution of Colombia's Drug Trade," InsightCrime: Organized Crime in the Americas. 3 December 2013. Internet: www.insightcrime.irg/news-analysis/20years-after-pablo-the-evolution-of-colomibias-drug-trade. Date accessed: 15 July 2015.
[224] Natasha Bertrand, "How 34 commandos created Mexico's most brutal drug cartel," Business Insider. 5 March 2015. Internet: www.businessinsider.com/how-34-commandos-created-mexicos-most-brutal-drug-cartel-2015-3. Date accessed: 15 July 2015.
[225] Helene Cooper and RukimiCallimachi, "Airstrikes kills a Deputy to IS Leader, U.S. says," The New York Times. 21 August 2015. Internet: http://www.nytimes.com/2015/08/22/world/middleeast/airstrike-kills-a-deputy-to-IS-leader. Date accessed: 24 August 2015.
[226] *Ibid.*
[227] Rowan Scarborough, "Killing Islamic State's leaders useless; `deep bench'

²²⁸replaces the dead," The Washington Times, 28 September 2015. Internet: http://www.washington times.com/news/2015/sep/28/Islamic-state-has-trained-operators. Date accessed: 5 October 2010.
²²⁸Jonathan Spyer, "IS: Can the West Win Without a Ground Game?," The Tower. October 2014. Internet: http://www.meforum.org/4846/IS-can-the-west-win-without-a-ground-game. Date accessed: 4 June 2015.
²²⁹Aymenn Jawad al-Tamimi, "America Should Aim to Contain, not Destroy, IS," The Huffington Post. 12 August 2015. Internet: http://www.meforum.org/5438/contain-IS. Date accessed: 17 August 2015.
²³⁰Rowan Scarborough, "Killing Islamic State's leaders useless; 'deep bench' replaces the dead," *op. cit.*
²³¹Anne Barnard and Tim Arango, "Using Violence and Persuasion, IS Makes Political Gains," *op. cit.*
²³²Glenn Greenwald, "Americans now fear ISIS sleeper cells are living in the US, overwhelmingly support military action," First Look. 8 September 2014. Internet: https://firstlook.org/theintercept/2014/09/08/lesson-americans-refuse-learn-war. Date accessed: 21 November 2014.
²³³Sabine Siebold, ParisaHafezi and Arshad Mohammed, U.S. to send special forces to Syria, truce sought after peace talks," Reuters. 30 October 2015. Internet: http://news.yahoo.com/iran-backs-six-month-syria-transition-ahead-peace-112939586.html. Date accessed: 2 November 2015.
²³⁴Anne Barnard and Tim Arango, "Using Violence and Persuasion, IS Makes Political Gains," *op. cit.*
²³⁵"Report: US-Trained, 'Vetted Moderate' Syrian Rebel Leader Defects to Al-Qaeda, Turns Weapons Over to Terror Group," PJ Media. 22 September 2015. Internet: http://pjmedia.com/tatler/2015/-0/22/report-u-s-trained-vetted-moderate-syrian-rebel. Date accessed: 23 September 2015.
²³⁶Aymenn Jawad al-Tamimi, "America Should aim to Contain, not Destroy IS," *op. cit.*
²³⁷Patrick Poole, "#BringBackOurRebels: Obama's 50-man 'Vetted Moderate' Syrian Rebel Army Vanishes After Training in Turkey," PJ Media.com. 29 July 2015. Internet: http://pjmedia.com/tatler/2015/07/27/cias-250-million-vetted-moderate-syrian-rebel. Date accessed: 29 July 2015.
²³⁸*Ibid.*
²³⁹"Report: US-Trained, 'Vetted Moderate' Syrian Rebel Leader Defects to Al Qaeda, Turns Weapons Over to Terror Group," PJ Media, *op. cit.*
²⁴⁰Kimiko De Freytas-Tamura, "Junaid Hussain, IS Recruiter, Reported Killed in Airstrike," *op. cit.*
²⁴¹Tarek Fatah, "War against IS Headed for Failure," The Toronto Sun, 16

September 2014. Internet: http://www.meforum.org/4821/war-against-IS-headed-for-failure. Date accessed: 4 June 2015.

²⁴²*Ibid.*

²⁴³ Tarek Fatah, "The Real Fight Against IS Begins in Saudi Arabia," The Toronto Sun, 27 January 2015. Internet: http://www.meforum.org/4995/shame-and-scandal-in-saudi-arabia. Date accessed: 4 June 2015.

²⁴⁴Tarek Fatah, "Saudi Arabia is Not our Friend." The Toronto Sun. 29 September 2015. Internet: http://www.meforum.org/5528/saudi-arabia-no-friend. Date accessed: 5 October 2015

²⁴⁵Fernando Betancor, "Outside the box: is the Islamic State close to victory?," Open Democracy. 10 September 2015. Internet: http://www.opendemocracy.net/arab-awakening/fernando-betancor/outside-box-is-islamic. Date accessed: 14 September 2015.

²⁴⁶ Tarek Fatah, "The Real Fight Against IS Begins in Saudi Arabia," *op. cit.*

²⁴⁷"Islamic State: The propaganda war," The Economist, 15 August 2015, *op. cit.*

²⁴⁸Abdel Bari Atwan, ""When it comes to `Islamic State,' the West just doesn't get it," *op. cit.*

²⁴⁹"Another Saudi Prince arrested, smuggling drugs for ISIS," Centre Star. 27 October 2015. Internet: http://thecentrestar.com/another-saudi-prince-arrested-smuggling-drugs-for-isis. Date accessed: 28 October 2015.

²⁵⁰Adam Withnall, "Saudi Arabia carried out 100ᵗʰ execution this year and is on course to set beheadings record," The Independent. 8 June 2015. Internet: www.independent.co.uk/news/world/middle-east/saudi-arabia-carries-out-100th-execution-this-year-and-is-on-course-toset-beheadings-record-10320995.html. Date accessed: 8 July 2015.

²⁵¹Tarek Fatah, "War against IS Headed for Failure," *op. cit.*

²⁵²Andrew Phillips, "The Islamic State's challenge to international order," *op. cit.*, p. 2.

²⁵³Can Erimtan, "The End of "Secular Turkey" or Ottomans re-emergent?" Russia Today. 13 January 2015. Internet: rt.com/op-edge/221835-turkey-religion-secular-state. Date accessed: 8 July 2015.

²⁵⁴Tarek Fatah, "War against IS Headed for Failure," *op. cit.*

²⁵⁵Daniel Pipes, "Turkey's Support for IS Islamist Terrorists," The Washington Times. 17 June 2014. Internet: http://www.meforum.org/4732/turkey-support-IS-iraq-syria. Date accessed: 4 June 2015.

²⁵⁶Daniel Pipes, "Did Turkish Intelligence Green-Light the Ankara Bombing?," National Review Online. 12 October 2015. Internet: http://meforum.org/5568/making-sense-of-the-ankara-bombing. Date accessed: 19 October 2015.

257 BurakBekdil, ""IS Going Rogue in Turkey, or Is It?" The Gatestone Institute. 4 August 2015. Internet: http:www.meforum.org/5422/turkey-IS. Date accessed: 6 August 2015.
258 *Ibid.*
259 *Ibid.*
260 BurakBekdil, " How Turkey Fights the Islamic State," The Gatestone Institute. 27 July 2015. Internet: http://www.meforum.org/5401/turkey-islamic-state. Date accessed: 29 July 2015.
261 *Ibid.*
262 BurakBekdil, "Turkey Turns on Its Jihadists Next Door," The Gatestone Institute. 28 July 2015. Internet: http://www.meforum.org/5406.turkey-vs-jihadists. Date accessed: 30 July 2015.
263 Aymenn Jawad al-Tamimi, "American Should Aim to Contain, not Destroy, IS," *op. cit.*
264 Daniel Pipes, "Turkey's Support for IS Islamist Terrorists," *op. cit.*
265 *Ibid.*
266 Alon Ben-Meir, "The Necessity of Iraqi Sunni Independence," Alon Ben-Meir.com. 10 June 2015. Internet: http://www.alonben-meir.com/article/the-necessity-of-iraqi-sunni-independence. Date accessed: 11 June 2015.
267 Anne Barnard and Tim Arango, "Using Violence and Political Persuasion, IS Makes Political Gains," *op. cit.*
268 Jonathan Spyer, "Dispatch from Iraq: Iran-backed Militias Keep IS at Bay, for a Price," The Australian. 4 July 2015. Internet: http://www.meforum.org/5365/iraq-iran-militia-IS. Date accessed: 8 July 2015.
269 Gordon and Schmitt, *op. cit.*
270 Jonathan Spyer, "IS: Can the West Win Without a Ground Game?" *op. cit.*
271 "Iran's Revolutionary Guard general killed in Syria amid IS attack," The Indian Express. 9 October 2015. Internet: http://indianexpress.com/article/world/middle-east-africa/revolutionary-guard-general. Date accessed: 12 October 2015.
272 Jonathan Spyer, "Dispatch from Iraq: The Stealth Iranian Takeover Becomes Clear," PJ Media. 31 July 2015. Internet: http://www.meforum.org/5412/iraq-iranian-takeover. Date accessed: 3 August 2015.
273 Ben Hubbard, "Offering services, IS Digs in Deeper in Seized Territories," *op. cit.*
274 Gordon and Schmitt, *op. cit.*
275 Michael Weiss and Hassan Hassan, ISIS: Inside the Army of Terror, *op. cit.*, p. 135.
276 "Syrian Army Makes Major Gains Against the Islamic State Amid

Setbacks in Aleppo," The Middle East Daily. 16 June 2015. Internet: http://link.foreignpolicy.com/view/52543e47c16cfa46f6cd22d2q14z.6rg/94725526. Date accessed: 17 June 2015.
[277] Gordon and Schmitt, *op. cit.*
[278] Jonathan Spyer, "Dispatch from Iraq: The Stealth Iranian Takeover Becomes Clear," *op. cit.*
[279] Murray, *op.cit.*
[280] *Ibid.*
[281] *Ibid.*
[282] *Ibid.*
[283] *Ibid.*
[284] Daniel Pipes, "IS Attacks on the West," The Washington Times, 22 May 2015. Internet: http://www.meforum.org/5255/IS-attacks-the-west. Date accessed: 4 June 2015.
[285] Ben-Meir, *op.cit.*
[286] Murray, *op.cit.*
[287] Ben-Meir, *op. cit.*
[288] Jonathan Spyer, "Dispatch from Iraq: Iran-Backed Militias Keep IS at Bay, for a Price," *op.cit.*
[289] *Ibid.*
[290] Quoted in Anne Barnard and Tim Arango, "Using Violence and Persuasion, IS Makes Political Gains," *op. cit.*
[291] *Ibid.*
[292] *Ibid.*
[293] Jim Muir, "Battle for Sinjar: IS-held town in Iraq 'liberated'," BBC. 13 November 2015. Internet: http://www.bbc.com/news/34806556. Date accessed: 15 November 2015.
[294] Ben-Meir, *op.cit.*
[295] *Ibid.*
[296] Jonathan Spyer, "Rival Peace Plans Won't Save Syria," The Jerusalem Post. 14 August 2015. Internet: http://www.meforum.org/5439/syria-peace-plans. Date accessed: 17 August 2015.
[297] Jamie Crawford, "U.S. warns Russia on military build-up in Syria," CNN. 10 September 2015. Internet: http://edition.cnn.com/2015/09/09/politics/russia-syria-military-buildup-kerry-lavrov/index.html. Date accessed: 12 September 2015.
[298] Jonathan Spyer, "Rival Peace Plans Won't Save Syria," *op. cit.*
[299] Jonathan Spyer, "Russia in Syria: Putin Fills Strategic Vacuum in the Middle East," The Australian. 3 October 2015. Internet: http://www.meforum.org/5537/russia-in-syria. Date accessed: 5 October 2015.
[300] Jonathan Wade, "Lavrov: Russia, U.S to Cooperate on Islamic State,"

Geopolitical Monitor. 30 September 2015. Internet: http://www.geopoliticalmonitor.com/lavrov-russia-u-s-to-cooperate-on-islamic-state. Date accessed: 6 October 2015.

[301] Jonathan Spyer, "Russia in Syria: Putin Fills Strategic Vacuum in the Middle East," *op. cit.*

[302] "What are Russian Airstrikes Aiming at in Syria?" Geopolitical Monitor. 7 October 2015. Internet: http://www.geopoliticalmonitor.com/what-are-the-russian-missiles-aimed-at-in-syria. Date accessed: 12 October 2015.

[303] Jonathan Spyer, "Russia in Syria: Putin Fills Strategic Vacuum in the in the Middle East," *op. cit.*

[304] "What are Russian Airstrikes Aiming at in Syria?" Geopolitical Monitor, *op. cit.*

[305] Ilan Berman, "Putin's Middle Eastern Moves," MEF Wires. 26 October 2015. Internet: http://www.meforum.org/5587/putin-middle-east. Date accessed: 28 October 2015.

[306] "Syria, Russia and the West: A game-changer in Latakia?," The Economist. 26 September -2 October 2015, p. 32.

[307] JonthanSpyer, "Russia in Syria: Putin Fills Strategic Vacuum in the Middle East," *op. cit.*

[308] David Blair, "Putin's plan for Syria is a war without end," The Sunday Times. 4 October 2015. Johannesburg, p. 17

[309] John Defterios, "ISIS: Can coalition cut off funding of world's wealthiest terror group?,*op. cit.*

[310] Michael Weiss and Hassan Hassan, ISIS: Inside the Army of Terror, *op. cit.*, p. 145.

[311] *Ibid.*, pp. 147-148.

[312] "Syria, Russia and the West: A game-changer in Latakia?," *op. cit.*

[313] David Blair, "Putin's plan for Syria is a war without end," *op. cit.*

[314] Jonathan Spyer, "Russia in Syria: Putin Fills Strategic Vacuum in the Middle East," *op. cit.*

[315] *Ibid.*

[316] *Ibid.*

[317] "Syria, Russia and the West: A game-changer in Latakia?," *op. cit.*

[318] Jonathan Wade, "Lavrov: Russia, U.S. to Cooperate on Islamic State," *op. cit.*

[319] Jonathan Spyer, "Russian Intervention in Syria Isn't a `Game Changer'," The Strategist. 30 October 2015. Internet: http://www.meforum.org/5601/russia-syria-not-gamechanger. Date accessed: 2 November 2015

[320] Jonathan Wade, "Lavrov: Russia, US to cooperate on Islamic State," *op. cit.*

[321] *Ibid.*

322Ilan Berman, "Putin's Middle Eastern Moves," *op. cit.*
323Jonathan Wade, "Lavrov: Russia, U.S. to cooperate on Islamic State," *op. cit.*
324Jonathan Spyer, "Russia in Syria: Putin Fills Strategic Vacuum in the Middle East," *op. cit.*
325*Ibid.*
326Jonathan Spyer, "Russian Intervention in Syria Isn't a `Game Changer'", *op. cit.*
327Almukhtar, *op. cit.*
328*Ibid.*
329Felix Imonti, "Islamic State Meets the Laws of Economics," Geopolitical Monitor. 22 October 2015. Internet: http://www.geopoliticalmonitor.com/islamic-state-meets-the-laws-of-economics. Date accessed: 27 October 2015.
330*Ibid.*
331Hubbard, *op. cit.*
332"Taliban warns IS not to interfere in Afghanistan," Mail and Guardian. 16 June 2015. Internet: http://mg.co.za/article/2015-06-16-taliban-warns-IS-not-to-interfere-in-afghanistan. Date accessed: 17 June 2015.
333*Ibid.*
334"Afghan Taliban denounce `brutal' IS execution video," The Indian Express. 11 August 2015. Internet: http://indianexpress.com/article/world/middle-east-africa/afghan-taliban-denounce-brutal. Date accessed: 12 August 2015.
335*Ibid.*
336Felix Imonti, "Islamic State Meets the Laws of Economics," Geopolitical Monitor. 22 October 2015. Internet: http://www.geopolliticalmonitor.com/islamic-state-meets-the-laws-of-economics. Date accessed: 27 October 2015.
337Anne Barnard and Tim Arango, "Using Violence and Persuasion, IS Makes Political Gains," *op. cit.*
338Aymenn Jawad Al-Tamimi, "The Evolution in Islamic State Administration: The Documentary Evidence," *op. cit.*
339Phyllis Chesler, "As IS Brutalizes Women, a Pathetic Feminist Silence, " The New York Post. 7 June 2015. Internet: http://www.meforum.org/5302/IS-feminist-silence. Date accessed: 10 June 2015.
340 Mark Durie, "Sex Slavery and the Islamic State," Online Opinion. 3 July 2015. Internet: http://www.meforum.org/5361/islamic-state-sex-slavery. Date accessed: 7 July 2015.
341"Libya Profile – Timeline, *op. cit.*
342Gal Luft, "Plan B for Libya," The American Interest. 1 October 2015.

Internet: http://www.meforum.org/5534/partition-libya. Date accessed: 5 October 2015.
[343] *Ibid.*
[344] "Libya appeals for help against IS group as Sirte falls," France 24. 17 August 2015. Internet: http://www.france24.com/en/20150817-libya-appeals-air-strikes-IS-islamic-state-group. Date accessed: 18 August 2015.
[345] "Libya fears Iraq-like IS scenario," *op. cit.*
[346] "Libya Profile – Timeline," *op. cit.*
[347] Ulf Laessing and Ayman al-Warfalli, "Expulsion from Derna bastion may show limits for Islamic State in Libya," Reuters. 24 July 2015. Internet: http://news.yahoo.com/expulsion-derna-bastion-may-show-limits-islamic-state-11364. Date accessed: 28 July 2015.
[348] *Ibid.*
[349] "Libya: IS begins new offensive on Derna," The North Africa Post. 11 August 2015. Internet: http://northafricapost.com/8756-libya-IS-begins-new-offensive-on-derna.html. Date accessed: 12 August 2015.
[350] Ulf Laessing and Ayman al-Warfalli, "Expulsion from Derna bastion may show limits for Islamic State in Libya," *op. cit.*
[351] "Libya: Tripoli bombs IS in Sirte," The North Africa Post. 23 June 2015. Internet: http://northafricapost.com/8104-libya-tripoli-bombs-is-in-sirte.html. Date accessed: 1 July 2015.
[352] "Black flags on Europe's doorstep: Inside IS' new capital Sirte on Libya's coast," Express. 16 August 2015. Internet: http://www.express.co.uk/news/world/598409/Sirte-IS-Libya-caliphate-capital. Date accessed: 17 August 2015
[353] *Ibid.*
[354] "Libya Profile – Timeline," *op. cit.*
[355] Laessing and al-Warfalli, *op. cit.*
[356] *Ibid.*
[357] "Libya appeals for help against IS group as Sirte falls," France 24, *op. cit.*
[358] "Libya Profile – Timeline," *op. cit.*
[359] "Libya appeals for help against IS group as Sirte falls," France 24, *op. cit.*
[360] Mustapha Tlili, "Saving Tunisia from IS," New York Times. 3 August 2015. Internet: http://www.nytimes.com/2015/08/04/opinion/saving-tunisia-from-IS.html. Date accessed: 5 August 2015.
[361] *Ibid.*
[362] Bruno, *op. cit.*
[363] *Ibid.*
[364] *Ibid.*
[365] Daniel Cohen and Danielle Levin, "How IS gained traction in the Middle East," *op. cit.*
[366] *Ibid.*

³⁶⁷Joseph S. Nye. "How to Fight the Islamic State," Khaosod English. 21 September 2015: Internet: http://www.khaosodenglish.com/detail.php?newsid=1442852185&section=200. Date accessed: 22 September 2015

³⁶⁸Hussein Solomon, Jihad: A South African Perspective, *op. cit.*, pp. 24-25.

³⁶⁹"Islamic State: The propaganda war," The Economist, 15 August 2015, *op. cit.*

³⁷⁰*Ibid.*

³⁷¹Joseph S. Nye. "How to Fight the Islamic State," Khaosod English. 21 September 2015, *op. cit.*

³⁷² Margaret Rouse, "What is a botnet (zombie army?," Definition from What Is.com. Internet: http:searchsecurity.techtarget.com/definition/botnet. Date accessed: 7 November 2015.

³⁷³"Islamic State: The propaganda war," The Economist, 15 August 2015, *op. cit.*

³⁷⁴Kimiko de Freytas-Tamura, "Junaid Hussain, IS Recruiter, Reported Killed in Airstrike," The New York Times, *op. cit.*

³⁷⁵*Ibid.*

³⁷⁶ "Islamic State: The propaganda war," The Economist. 15 August 2015, *op. cit.*

³⁷⁷Elizabeth Whitman, "Islamic State Recruitment: IS Seeks Fighters From Caucasus, Central Asia and Indonesia", *op. cit.*

³⁷⁸EbrahimMoosa, "My madrassa classmate hated politics, then joined IS," *op. cit.*

³⁷⁹Hussein Solomon, Terrorism and Counter-Terrorism in Africa: Fighting Insurgency from Al Shabaab, Ansar Dine and Boko Haram. Palgrave Macmillan. London. 2015, pp. 135-136.

³⁸⁰Azizur R. Patel, "De-Islamizing Politics and Society in the MENA Region," RIMA Occasional Papers, Vol. 1 No. 19, August 2013, p. 2. Internet: https://muslimsinafrica.wordpress.com/2013/08/27/de-islamizing-politics-and-society-in-the-mena-region-azizur-rahman-patel. Date accessed: 6 November 2015.

³⁸¹Cawo Abdi, "The identity crisis of 21st century Muslims," CNN. 24 August 2015. Internet: htpp://edition.cnn.com/2015/08/24/opinions/islam-identity-crIS-cawo-abdi. Date accessed: 25 August 2015.

³⁸²Abdel Bari Atwan, "When it comes to `Islamic State,' the West just doesn't get it," *op. cit.*

³⁸³Bobby Gosh, "Mission Possible: To combat the lure of ISIL, the Muslim world needs its own Peace Corps," QZ Bulletin. 23 October 2015. Internet: http://qz.com/530734/to-combat-the-lure-of-isil-the-muslim-world-needs-

its-own-peace-corps. Date accessed: 26 October 2015.
[384]Tausch, *op. cit.*, p. 4.
[385]"Islamic extremism: The battle of ideas," The Economist, 15-21 August 2015, p. 25.
[386]*Ibid.*
[387]Kimiko de Freytas-Tamura, "Junaid Hussain, IS Recruiter, Reported Killed in Airstrike," The New York Times, *op. cit.*
[388]Pankaj Mishra, "How to think about Islamic State," The Guardian, 24 July 2015. Internet: http://www.theguardian.com/books/2015/jul/24/how-to-think-about-islamic-state. Date accessed: 28 July 2015.
[389]"Islamic State: The propaganda war," The Economist, 15 August 2015, *op. cit.*
[390]Fernando Betancor, "Outside the box: is Islamic State close to victory?," *op. cit.*
[391]Gregory Tomlin, *op. cit.*
[392]Felix Arteaga, "The European Union's role in the fight against ISIS," European Leadership Network. 30 September 2014. Internet: http://www.europeanleadershipnetwork.org/the-european-unions-role-in-the-fight-against-isis_1955.html. Date accessed: 25 November 2014.
[393]*Ibid.*
[394]"Anonymous declares cyber war on ISIS Twitter users," Russia Today. 11 April. 2015. Internet: https://www.rt.com/news/248845-anonymous-opisis-warring-terrorism. Date accessed: 20 October 2015.
[395]*Ibid.*
[396]*Ibid.*
[397]Anthony Cuthbertson, "Anonymous affiliates GhostSec thwarts Isis terror plots in New York and Tunisia," IB Times. 22 July 2015. Internet: http://www.ibtimes.co.uk/anonymous-affiliate-ghostsec-thwarts-isis-terror-plots-new-york-tunisia-1512031. Date accessed: 20 October 2015.
[398]*Ibid.*
[399]Colin Freeman, "South African mercenaries' secret war on Boko Haram," The Telegraph. 10 May 2015. Internet: http://www.telegraph.co.uk/news/worldnews/africaandindianocean/nigeria/11596210/South-African-mercenaries-secret-war-on-Boko-Haram.html. Date accessed: 20 October 2015.
[400]*Ibid.*
[401]David Smith, "South Africa' ageing white mercenaries who helped turn tide on Boko Haram," The Guardian. 14 April 2015. Internet: http://www.theguardian.com/world/2015/apr/14/south-africas-ageing-white-mercenaries-who-helped-turn-tide-on-boko-haram. Date accessed: 20 October 2015.

⁴⁰²Colin Freeman, "South African mercenaries' secret war on Boko Haram," *op. cit.*
⁴⁰³David Smith, "South Africa's ageing white mercenaries who helped turn tide on Boko Haram," *op. cit.*
⁴⁰⁴Hussein Solomon, Terrorism and Counter-Terrorism in Africa: Fighting Insurgency from Al Shabaab, Ansar Dine and Boko Haram. Palgrave-Macmillan. London, pp. 108-112.
⁴⁰⁵Colin Freeman, "South African mercenaries' secret war on Boko Haram," *op. cit.*
⁴⁰⁶Murray Weidenbaum, "The role of business in fighting terrorism," Business Horizons. May-June 2003. Internet: https://news.wustl.edu/Document/wiedenbaum-biz.terror.pdf. Date accessed: 20 October 2015, p. 6.
⁴⁰⁷Stacy Reiter Neal, "Business as usual? Leveraging the Private Sector to Combat Terrorism," Perspective on Terrorism.Vol. 2 No. 3, 2008. Internet: http://www.terrorismananalysts.com/pt/index.php/pot/article/view/31/html. Date accessed: 20 October 2015.
⁴⁰⁸Hussein Solomon, Jihad: A South African Perspective. Sun Media. Bloemfontein, 2013, p. 74.
⁴⁰⁹Murray Weidenbaum, "The role of business in fighting terrorism," *op. cit.*
⁴¹⁰*Ibid.*
⁴¹¹*Ibid.*
⁴¹²Stacy Reiter Neal, "Business as usual? Levaraging the Private Sector to Combat Terrorism," *op. cit.*
⁴¹³*Ibid.*
⁴¹⁴*Ibid.*
⁴¹⁵Aymenn Jawad Al-Tamimi, "The Evolution in State Administration: The Documentary Evidence," *op. cit.*
⁴¹⁶*Ibid.*
⁴¹⁷Tarek Fatah, "Tackling Islamism, Post-Chattanooga," *op. cit.*
⁴¹⁸John Defterios, "ISS: Can coalition cut off funding of world's wealthiest terror group?" *op. cit.*
⁴¹⁹*Ibid.*
⁴²⁰*Ibid.*
⁴²¹Hussein Solomon, "Jihad: A South African Perspective. Sun Press. Bloemfontein. 2013, p. 46.
⁴²²*Ibid.*
⁴²³Rowan Scarborough, "Killing Islamic State's leaders useless; 'deep bench' replaces the dead," *op. cit.*
⁴²⁴*Ibid.*
⁴²⁵*Ibid.*
⁴²⁶*Ibid.*

427 Jonathan Spyer, "Russia in Syria: Putin Fills Strategic Vacuum in the Middle East," *op.cit.*
428 David A. Patten, "Defeating ISIS, Rolling Back Iran," Middle East Quarterly. Fall 2015. Internet: http://www.meforum.org/5479/defeating-isis-rolling-back-iran. Date accessed: 7 October 2015.
429 *Ibid.*
430 Jonathan Wade, "Lavrov: Russia, US to Cooperate on Islamic State," *op. cit.*
431 *Ibid.*
432 "Syria, Russia and the West: A game-changer in Latakia?," *op. cit.*
433 Fernando Betancor, "Outside the box: Is the Islamic State close to victory?," *op. cit.*
434 *Ibid.*
435 Daniel Pipes, "Why the Paris Massacre will have Limited Impact," *op. cit.*
436 Jon Stone, "Isis in the Middle East: Dozens of UK families beg police for help stopping relatives traveling to Syria," The Independent. 17 October 2014. Internet: http://www.independent.co.uk/news/uk/crime/isis-in-the-middle-east-dozens-of-uk-families-beg-police-for-help-stopping-relatives-traveling-to-syria-9801102.html. Date accessed: 24 November 2014.
437 *Ibid.*
438 Sabine Siebold, ParisaHafezi and Arshad Mohammed, "U.S. to send special forces to Syria, truce sought after peace talks," Reuters. 30 October 2015, *op. cit.*
439 David E. Sanger, "Agreement Reached to Restart Syria Peace Talks and Seek Cease-Fire," The New York Times. 30 October 2015. Internet: http://www.nyimes.com/2015/10/31/world/middleeast/agreement-reached-to-restart-syria-peace-talks-and-seek-cease-fire.html. Date accessed: 2 November 2015.
440 Fernando Betancor, "Outside the box: Is the Islamic State close to victory", *op. cit.*
441 Rowan Scarborough, "Killing Islamic State's leaders useless; `deep bench' replaces the dead," *op. cit.*
442 Katie Zavadski, "ISIS now has a network of military affiliates in 11 countries around the world," NYMAG. 23. November 2014. Internet: http://nymag.com/daily/intelligencer/2014/11/isis-now-has-military-allies-in-11-countries.html. Date accessed: 25 November 2014.
443 Olivia McCoy, "Islamic State Calls for Al Shabaab to Pledge Allegiance," Centre for Security Policy. 22 May 2015. Internet: https://www.centreforsecuritypolicy.org/2015/05/22/islamic-state-calls-for-al-shabaab-t0-pledge-allegiance. Date accessed: 9 November 2015.
444 Abdel Bari Atwan, "When it comes to `Islamic State,' the West just doesn't get it," *op. cit.*

⁴⁴⁵Rowan Scarborough, "Killing Islamic State's leaders useless; `deep bench' replaces the dead," *op. cit.*
⁴⁴⁶Robin Simcox, 'We Will Conquer Your Rome': A Study of Islamic State's Terrorism Plots in the West. Centre for the Response to Radicalization and Terrorism, Henry Jackson Society. London. 2015, p. 3.
⁴⁴⁷Alessandria Masi, "ISIS, aka Islamic State, Warns of Sleeper Cell Attacks on US interests in retaliation for bombings," IB Times. 8 August 2015. Internet: http://www.ibtimes.com/isis-aka-islamic-state-warns-sleeper-cell-attacks-us-interests-retaliation-bombings-1653437. Date accessed: 1 December 2014.
⁴⁴⁸Nico Hines, "Crackdown: To Stop ISIS, Britain is set to Stop Free Speech," The Daily Beast. 25 November 2014. Internet: http://www.thedailybeast.com/articles/2014/11/25/to-stop-isis-britain-is-set-to-stop-free-speech.html. Date accessed: 26 November 2014.
⁴⁴⁹Thomas Jocelynn, "Islamic State video congratulates Sinai `province' for downing Russian airliner" Threat Matrix: A Blog of the Long War Journal. 6 November 2015. Internet: http://longwarjournal.org/archives/2015/11/islamic-state-video-congratulates-sinai-province-for-downing-russian-airliner.php. Date accessed: 9 November 2015.
⁴⁵⁰"Day of mourning in Lebanon after deadly Beirut bombings," Al Jazeera. 13 November 2015. Internet: http://www.aljazeera.com/news/2015/11/isil-claims-suicide-bombing-southern-beirut-151112193802793.html. Date accessed: 15 November 2015.
⁴⁵¹Paul Ingram, "Crowds gather for anti-Islam demonstration outside Phoenix mosque," Reuters. 30 May 2015. Internet: http://www.reuters.com/article/2015/05/30/us-usa-islam-cartoon-idUSKBN0OE23320150530. Date accessed: 9 July 2015.
⁴⁵² Mark Durie, "Sex Slavery and the Islamic State," Online Opinion. 3 July 2015, *op. cit.*
⁴⁵³Williams, *op. cit.*, p. 1
⁴⁵⁴ManasiGopalkrishnan, "An interview of Dr. Moshe Terdiman on Deutsche Welle (DW) on the Muslim Population by 2050," Internet: https://muslimsinafrica.wordpress.com/2015/04/08/an-interview-of-dr-moshe-terdiman-on-deutsche-welle-dw-on-the-muslim-population-by-2050. Date accessed: 21 April 2015.
⁴⁵⁵ Colin Freeman, "Nigeria's descent into holy war," The Daily Telegraph, 8 January 2015. Internet: http://www.telegraph.co.uk/new/worldnews/africaandindianocean/nigeria89999758/N. Date accessed: 9 January 2015.
⁴⁵⁶Eric Kaufmann, Shall the Religious Inherit the Earth? Demography and

Politics in the Twenty-First Century. Profile Books. London, 2010.
[457]*Ibid.*, p. xvi.

www.ingramcontent.com/pod-product-compliance
Lightning Source LLC
Chambersburg PA
CBHW070549090426
42735CB00013B/3116